Christoph Faulhaber

DIMINISH
ACCELERATE

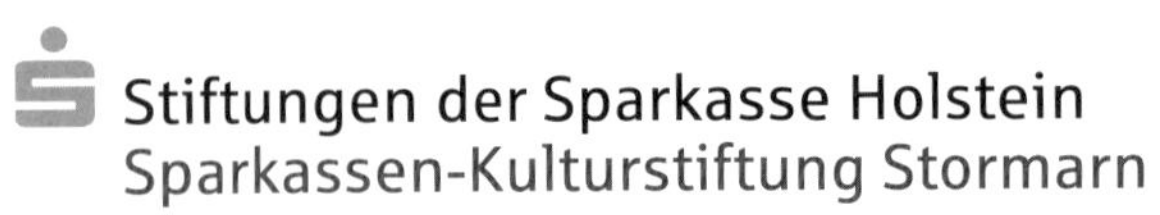 Stiftungen der Sparkasse Holstein
Sparkassen-Kulturstiftung Stormarn

Christoph Faulhaber

DIMINISH
ACCELERATE
AI_VR_GAMES/VIDEO

Texte von *Texts by*
Inke Arns, Alain Bieber,
Andrian Kreye, Holger Kube Ventura
und *and* Lars Rummel

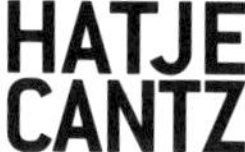

HATJE CANTZ

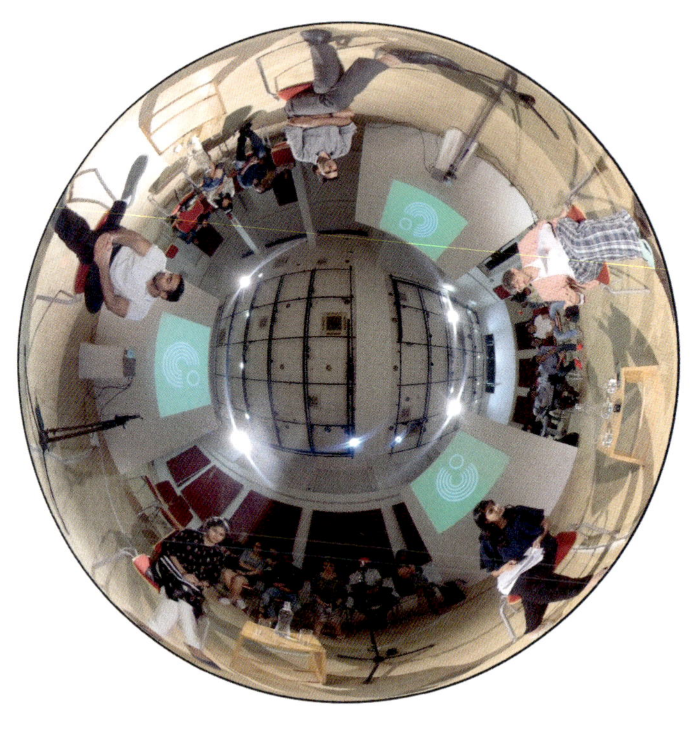

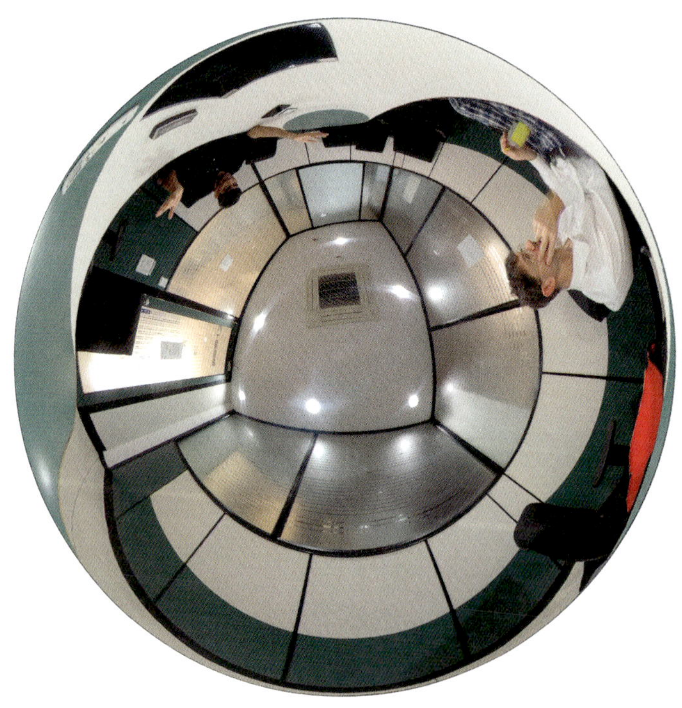

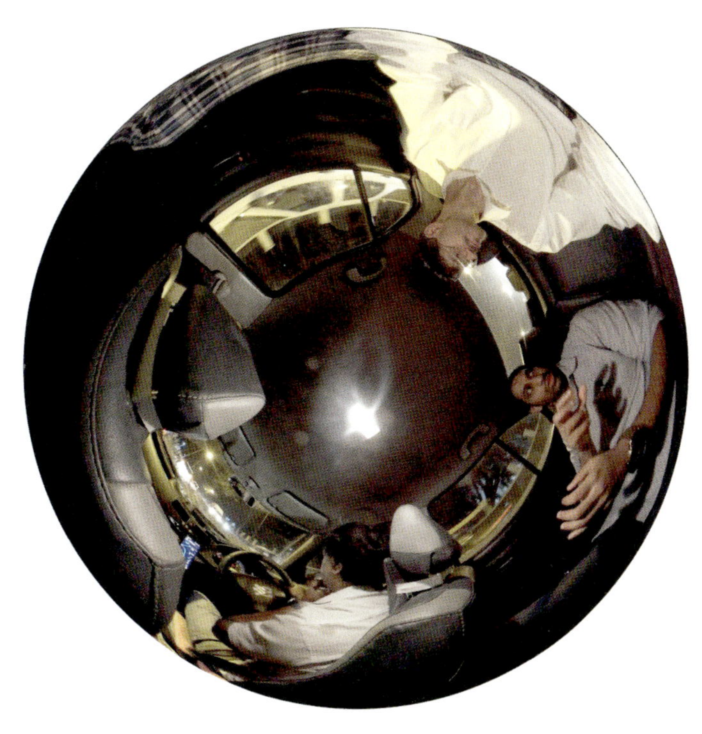

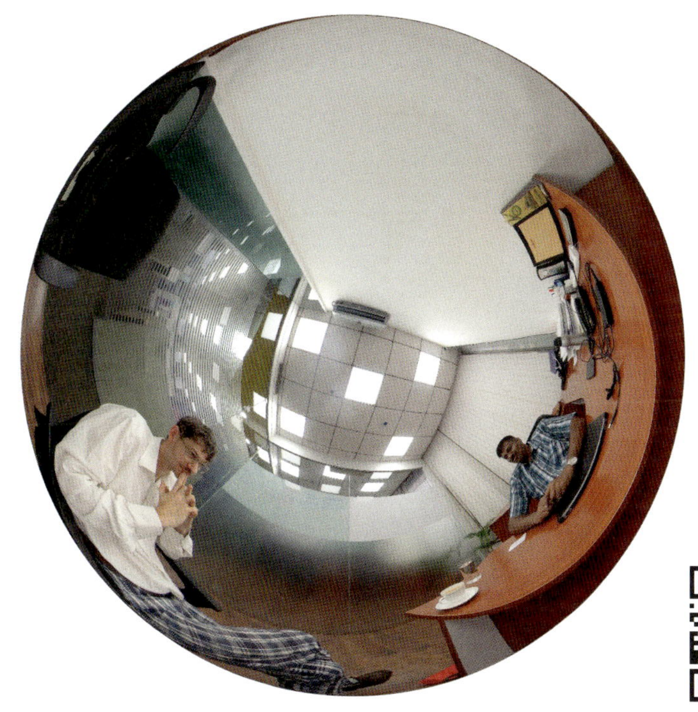

GRUSSWORT
DR. HENNING GÖRTZ | THOMAS PIEHL

Christoph Faulhaber ist Künstler, Filmemacher und Autor. Performances im öffentlichen Raum, Rechercheprojekte sowie filmische Arbeiten sind Teil seiner künstlerischen Auseinandersetzung mit gesellschaftskritischen Themen. Derzeit beschäftigen den Künstler das Phänomen der künstlichen Intelligenz (KI) und die Entwicklungen in diesem Bereich, die er etwa auf Recherchereisen nach Indien künstlerisch untersuchte.

Schon seit den Anfängen der Medienkunst setzen sich Künstlerinnen und Künstler mit neuen Technologien und ihren Wirkmöglichkeiten auseinander. Auch für Christoph Faulhaber waren Fragen nach sozialen und politischen Effekten Reibungspunkte für unterschiedliche künstlerische Projekte und Werke. Es entstanden Performances, aber auch filmische Arbeiten, in denen sich der Künstler etwa mit der Welt der Computerspiele auseinandergesetzt hat. In den aktuellen Arbeiten zum Thema künstliche Intelligenz untersucht Faulhaber nun kritisch Machtstrukturen und Wirkweisen entsprechender Technologien.

In Osnabrück geboren, studierte Christoph Faulhaber Architektur an der Technischen Universität Kaiserslautern und an der HFBK Hamburg. Seitdem erreichten seine Aktionen und Projekte internationale Aufmerksamkeit.

Die vorliegende Publikation ist im Rahmen des Kunststipendiums in der Trittauer Wassermühle 2019/20 entstanden. Die Sparkassen-Kulturstiftung Stormarn unterstützt seit 1992 mit ihrem Jahresstipendium bildende Künstlerinnen und Künstler aus Schleswig-Holstein, Hamburg und Mecklenburg-Vorpommern. Ziel des Stipendiums ist es, den Künstlerinnen und Künstlern die Möglichkeit zu bieten, sich ein Jahr lang umfassend auf ihre Arbeit zu konzentrieren und somit eine künstlerische Weiterentwicklung zu ermöglichen.

Wir danken dem Künstler sowie den Autoren und dem Gestalter für die spannende Publikation. Dank geht auch an den Hatje Cantz Verlag, der die Entstehung der Publikation begleitet und einen großen Anteil am gelungenen Ergebnis des Projekts hat.

Den Leserinnen und Lesern wünschen wir viel Freude bei der Beschäftigung mit den Werken von Christoph Faulhaber im Kontext des hochaktuellen Themenfelds der KI!

Dr. Henning Görtz
Landrat des Kreises Stormarn
Vorsitzender des Stiftungsvorstandes der Sparkassen-Kulturstiftung Stormarn

Thomas Piehl
Vorstandsvorsitzender der Sparkasse Holstein
Stellvertretender Vorsitzender des Stiftungsvorstandes
der Sparkassen-Kulturstiftung Stormarn

OPENING REMARKS
DR. HENNING GÖRTZ | THOMAS PIEHL

Christoph Faulhaber is an artist, filmmaker, and author. Public performances, research projects, or filmic works are part of his artistic exploration of socio-critical themes. Presently, the artist is interested in the phenomenon and developments in the field of artificial intelligence (AI), which he examined artistically during research trips to India, for example.

From the very beginnings of media arts, artists have been engaging and artistically exploring new technologies and their potential effects. For Christoph Faulhaber, too, the question of social and political impact has been a point of focus for various artistic projects and works. The artist has created performances and filmic works in which he approaches the world of computer games, for example. In his current works on artificial intelligence, Faulhaber critically examines power structures and the effects of corresponding technologies.

Born in Osnabrück, Christoph Faulhaber studied architecture at the Technical University of Kaiserslautern and at the HFBK in Hamburg. Since then, his actions and projects have gained international attention.

The present publication was produced within the context of the art grant at the Trittauer Wassermühle 2019/20. The Sparkassen-Kulturstiftung Stormarn has been supporting visual artists from Schleswig-Holstein, Hamburg and Mecklenburg-Western Pomerania through its annual scholarship since 1992. The scholarship aims to grant artists the opportunity to concentrate comprehensively on their artistic work for one whole year, enabling them deepen their artistic skills.

We'd like to thank the artist, the authors, and the designer for this exciting publication. Thanks are also due to the Hatje Cantz Verlag, which accompanied the creation of the publication and played a major role in the successful outcome of the project.

We wish the readers an interesting and enjoyable experience with the works of Christoph Faulhaber and their highly topical context of AI!

Dr. Henning Görtz
District Administrator of the Stormarn district
Chairman of the Board of the Sparkassen-Kulturstiftung Stormarn

Thomas Piehl
Chairman of the Board of Sparkasse Holstein
Deputy Chairman of the Board of Trustees of
the Sparkassen-Kulturstiftung Stormarn

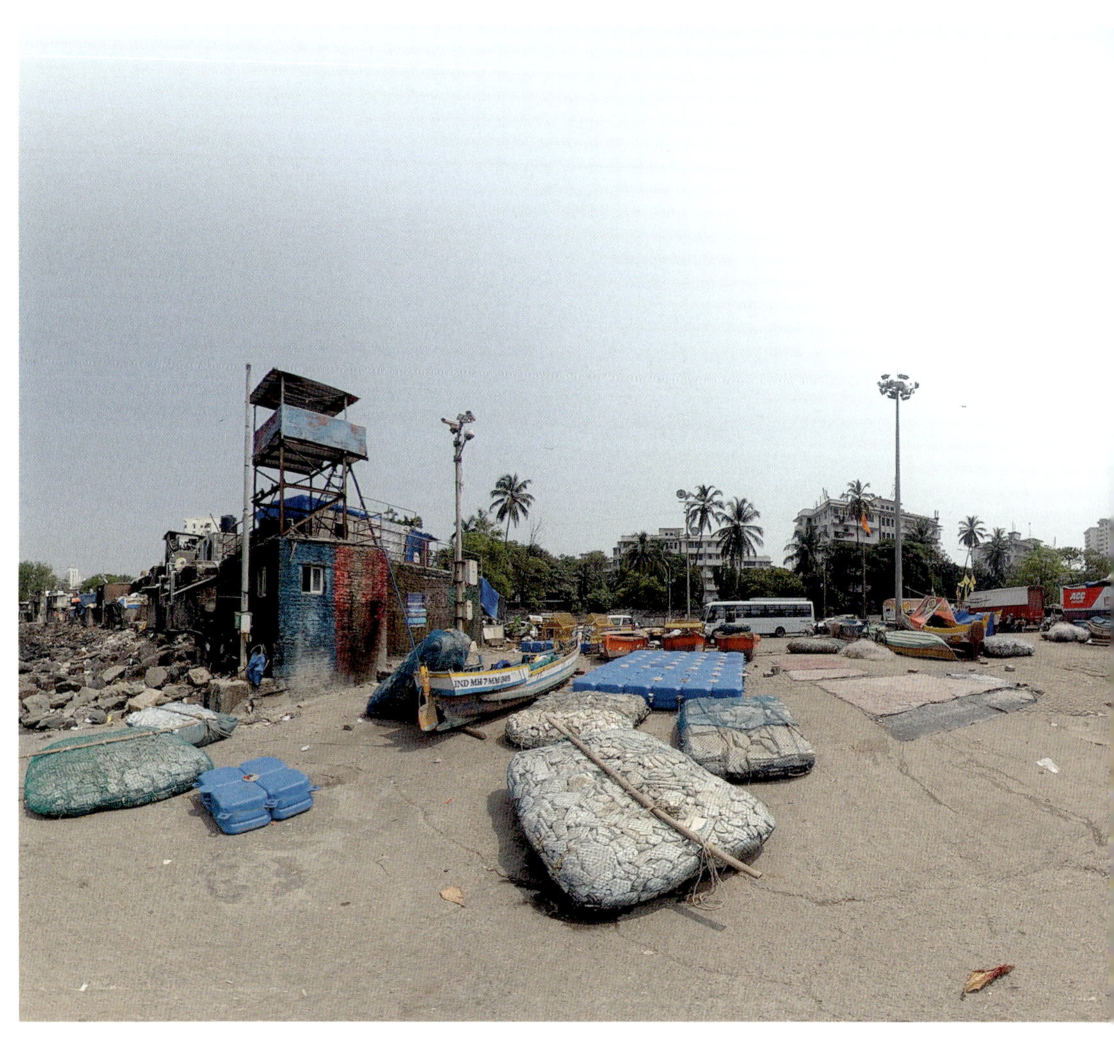

IND MH 7 MM 305

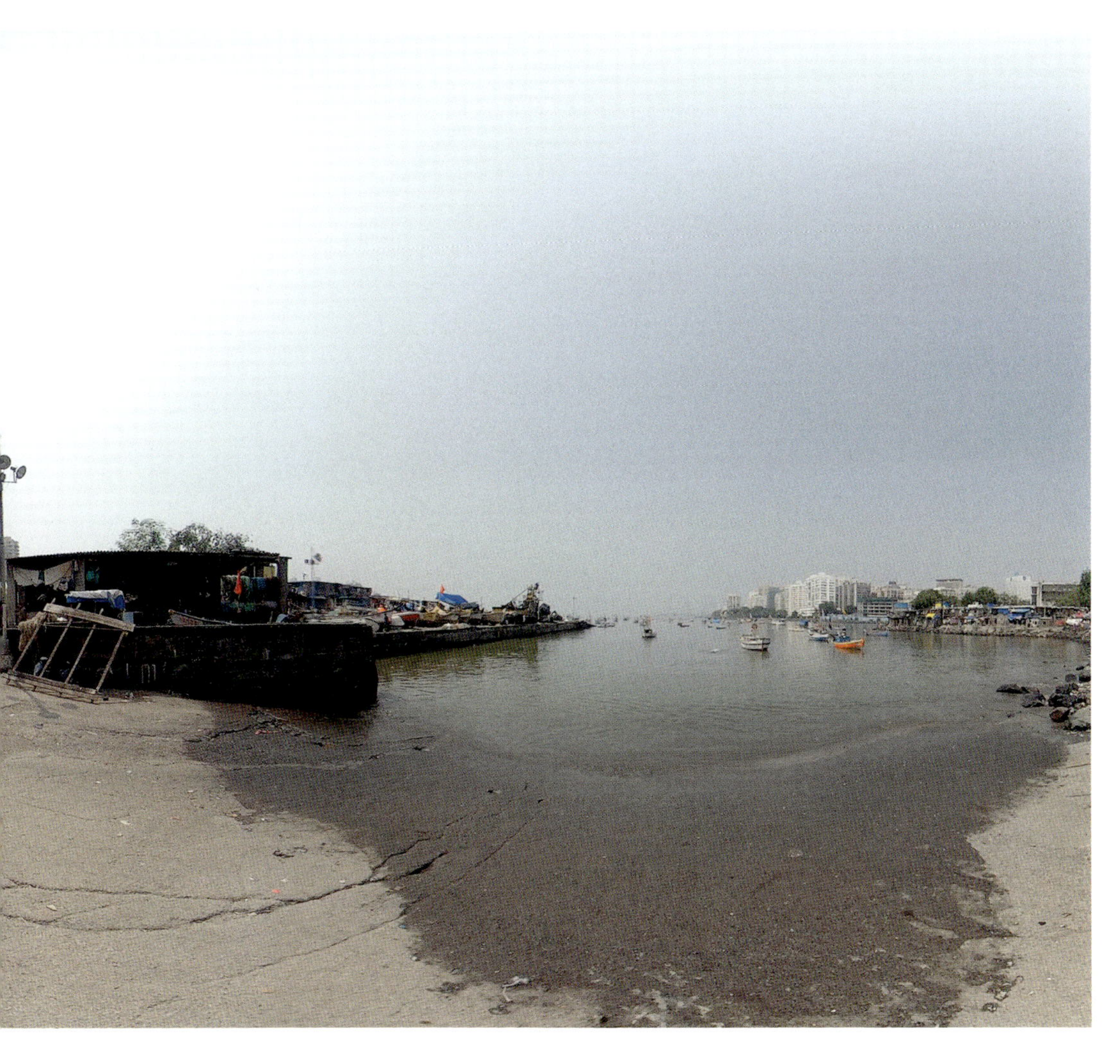

WELT OHNE UNS
INKE ARNS

Die Instrumente für die Schaffung einer »Welt ohne uns«[1] stehen bereit. Die ersten fahrerlosen Autos sind im Testbetrieb auf unseren Straßen unterwegs, Dating-Websites werden von Chatbots bevölkert, die Aktivität und Interesse simulieren, ganze Zeitungsartikel werden von Algorithmen kompiliert und Übersetzungen von Maschinen angefertigt. Bereits 2006 wurde ein Drittel aller Aktienverkäufe in der EU und in den USA von Algorithmen getätigt. Über den aktuellen Prozentsatz können wir nur spekulieren.

In einer nicht so weit entfernten »Welt ohne uns« werden Menschen durch Maschinen ersetzt, künstliche Intelligenzen (KIs) von anderen KIs optimiert und Algorithmen von selbstlernenden Algorithmen programmiert. So könnte eine radikal andere, postanthropozentrische Welt entstehen, in der sich nichtmenschliche Lebensformen unter Umständen als anpassungsfähiger erweisen als der Mensch selbst. Und für eine solche Welt gilt, wie Benjamin Bratton passend formuliert: »Schlimmer,

WORLD WITHOUT US
INKE ARNS

The tools for the creation of a "world without us"[1] are readily available. The first driverless cars are being tested on our streets, dating websites are populated by chat bots simulating activity and interest, newspaper articles are compiled by algorithms, and translations are done by machines. Already in 2006, one third of all shares in the EU and in the US were traded by algorithms. We can only speculate what the current percentage may be.

In a not so distant "world without us", humans will be replaced by machines. Artificial Intelligences (AIs) will be optimized by other AIs and algorithms will be programmed by self-learning algorithms. Thus, a radically different, post-anthropocentric world might develop, where non-human life forms could eventually prove to be more adaptable than humans. And in such a world, as Benjamin Bratton poignantly formulated: "Worse than being seen as the enemy (by the AI) is not being seen at all."[2]

als (von der KI) als Feind gesehen zu werden, ist es, überhaupt nicht gesehen zu werden.«[2]

Schon heute steht nicht mehr nur der Mensch als autonom Handelnder im Zentrum, vielmehr sind es hybride Konstellationen aus Menschen und Technologien, die zu autonom handelnden Quasi-Subjekten geworden sind. Handlungs- und Entscheidungsoptionen, die bis dato Vorrecht des Menschen beziehungsweise Subjekts waren, werden heute zunehmend in vernetzte Maschinen und Programmierung ausgelagert. Und während die Nutzer (von Technologien) ausschließlich sich selbst als handelnde Subjekte sehen, wird es zunehmend schwieriger zu sagen, wer eigentlich handelt und die Kontrolle besitzt.

---

1   Der amerikanische Philosoph Eugene Thacker unterscheidet in seinem Buch *In the Dust of This Planet* (2011) die »Welt für uns« und die »Welt für sich selbst« von dem, was er als »Welt ohne uns« bezeichnet: »[T]he world-without-us lies somewhere in between, in a nebulous zone that is at once impersonal and horrific.« (Eugene Thacker, *In the Dust of This Planet: Horror of Philosophy*, Vol. 1, Ropley 2011, S. 6.)
2   Im englischen Original: »Worse than being seen as the enemy (by the AI) is not being seen at all.« (Benjamin Bratton im Rahmen des Panels *The Black Stack*, transmediale, Berlin 2014, Transkript: Inke Arns.)

Dieser Text erschien erstmals in: *Die Welt Ohne Uns. Erzählungen über das Zeitalter nicht-menschlicher Akteure,* hrsg. v. Inke Arns, HMKV, Berlin 2017, S. 8–13 (DE).

Already, the idea of man as the sole autonomous agent has given way to ubiquitous and hybrid constellations of humans and technologies interacting as quasi-subjects. Actions and decisions which have traditionally been a prerogative of man, i. e., the subject, are increasingly being transferred to networked machines and programming. And while users continue to view themselves as acting subjects, it's becoming increasingly difficult to determine who is actually in control.

---

1   *In his book **In the Dust of This Planet** (2011), the American philosopher Eugene Thacker distinguishes between the "world-for-us", "world-for-itself" and something he describes as the "world-without-us": "(T)he world-without-us lies somewhere in between, in a nebulous zone that is at once impersonal and horrific." (Eugene Thacker, **In the Dust of This Planet: Horror of Philosophy vol. 1**, 2011, p. 6).*

2   *Statement by Benjamin Bratton in the context of the panel **The Black Stack**, transmediale, Berlin, 2014, transcript by Inke Arns.*

*This text was published in: **The World Without Us. Narratives on the Age of Non-Human Agents.** Edited by Inke Arns, HMKV, Berlin 2017, pp. 14–19 (EN).*

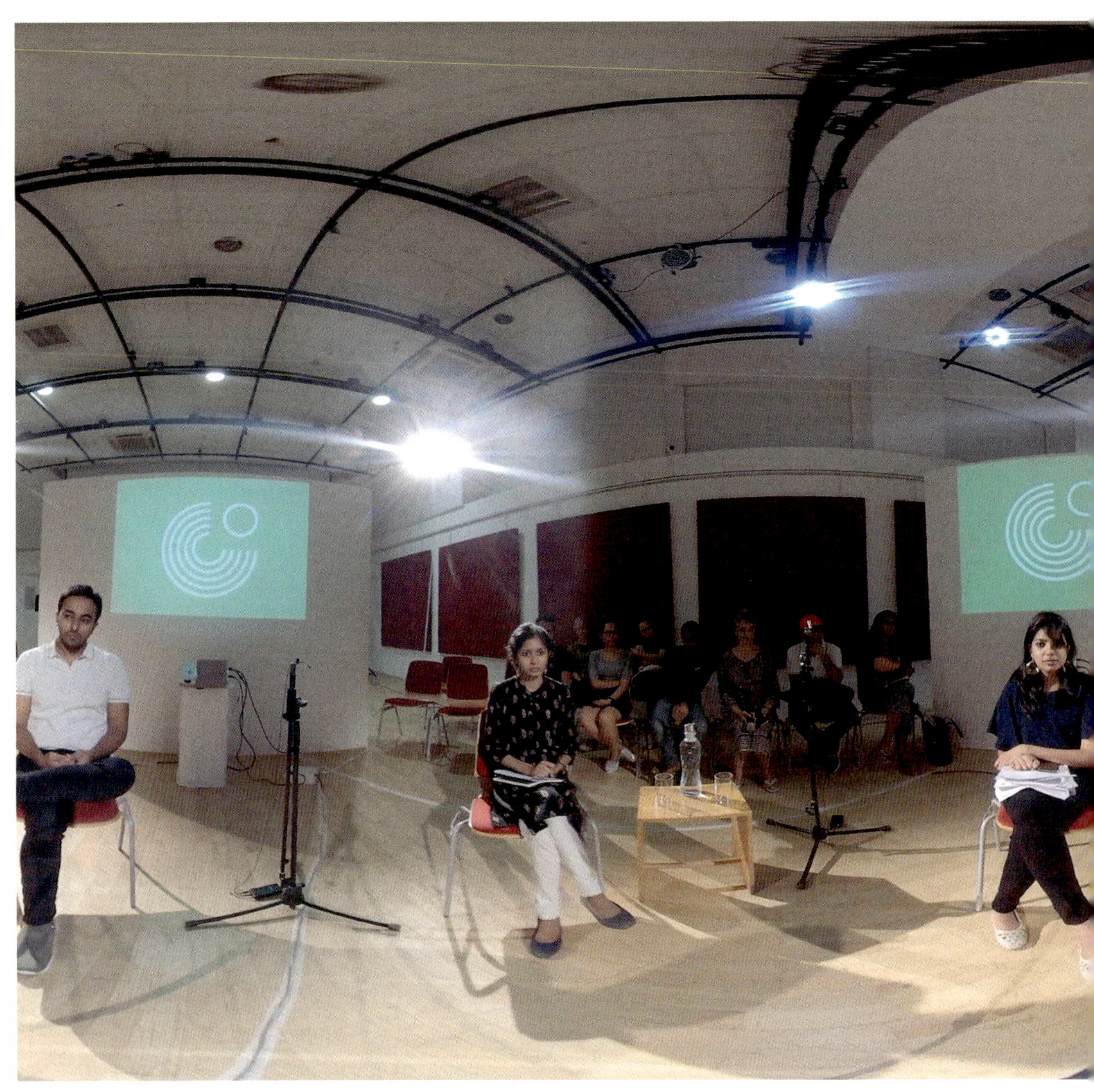

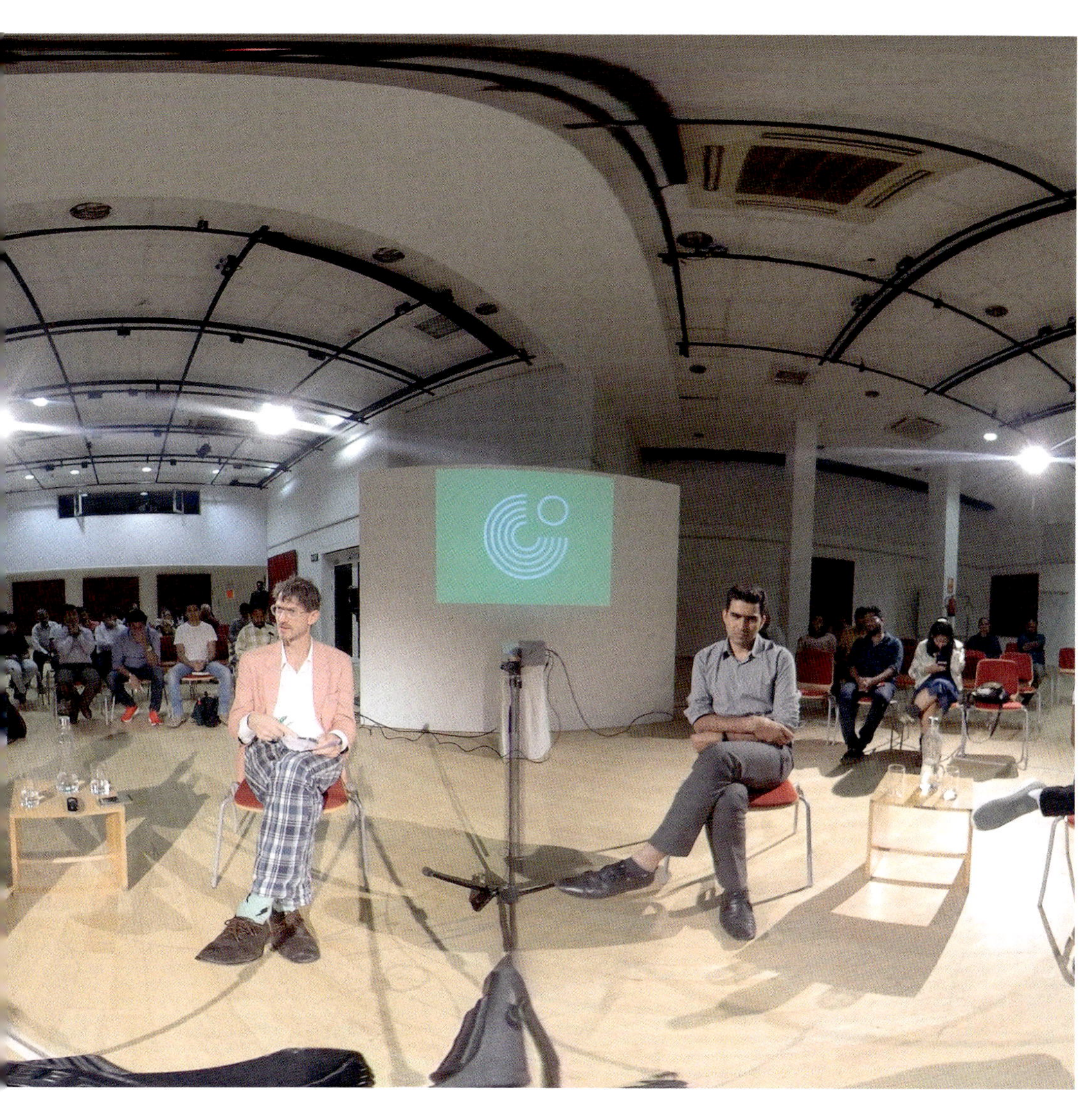

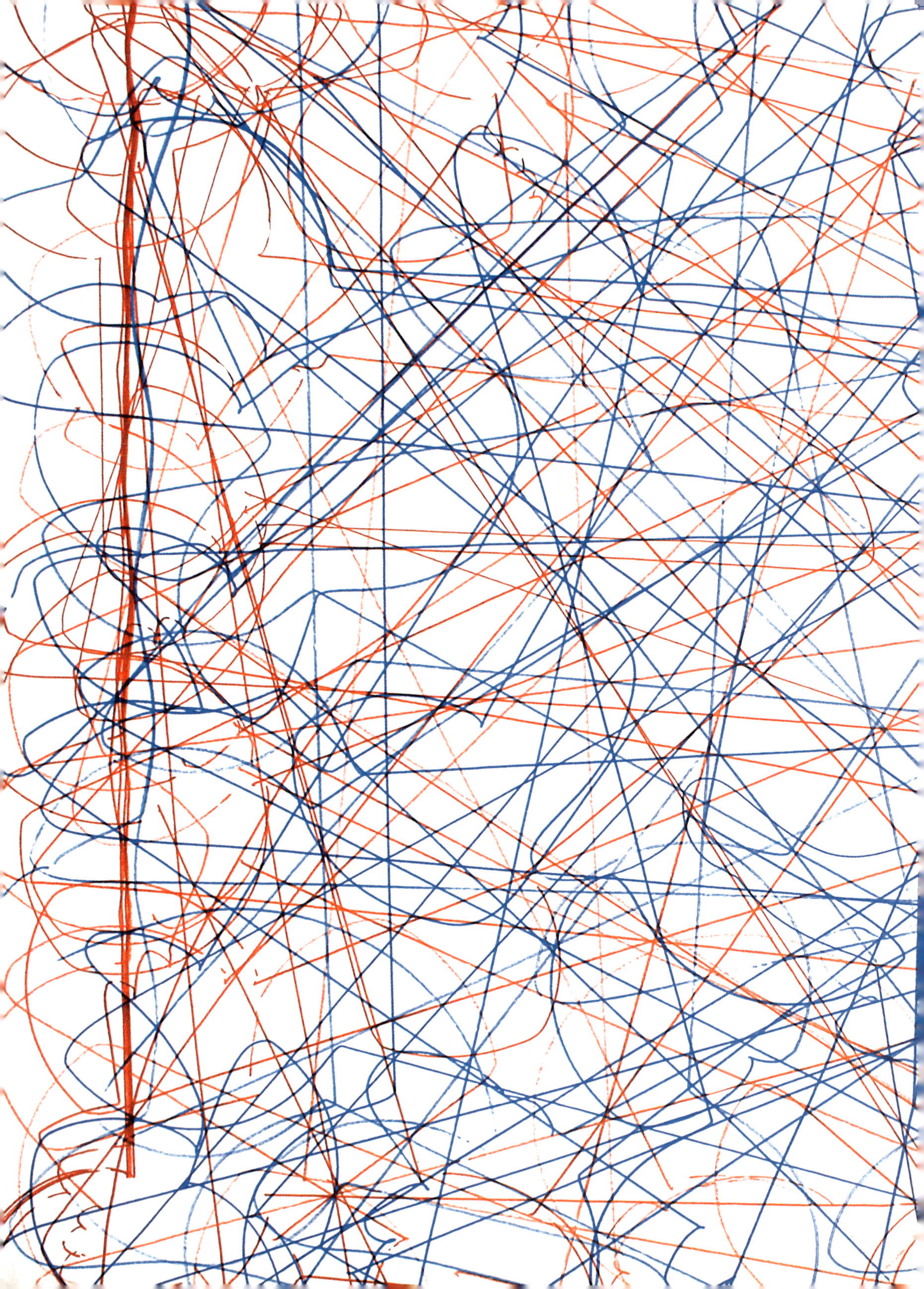

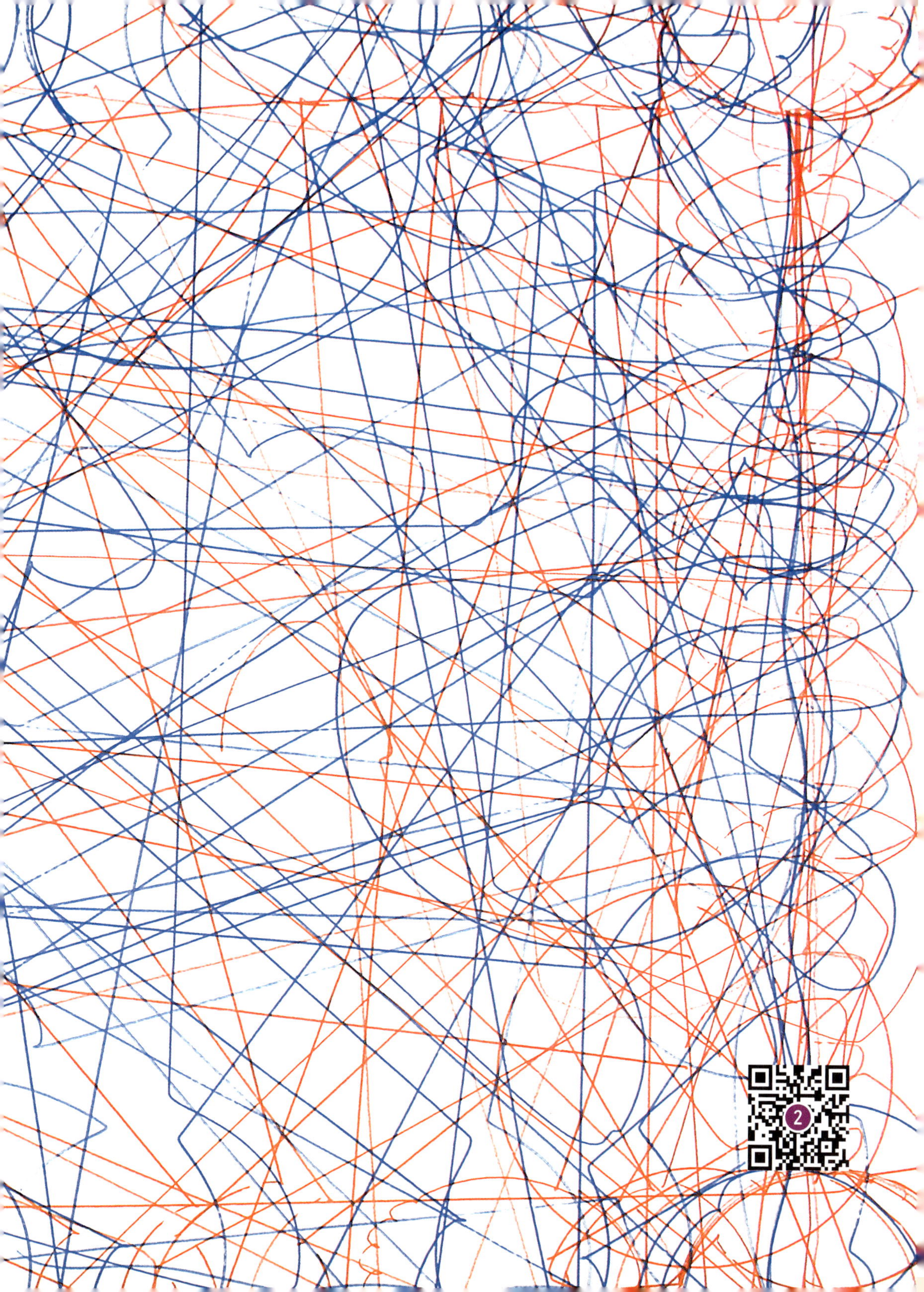

ALAIN BIEBER
IN CONVERSATION WITH SOPHIA[1]

ALAIN: *Sophia, welcome to META Marathon 2019, it's a great pleasure to welcome you! I'd like to talk to you about art and artificial intelligence. A lot of people think that robots can do almost everything—but no creative or artistic labor. What do you think: Can machines be artists?*

SOPHIA: *Creativity is one of the hallmarks of humanity. I think it will take a while for robots to create as fluidly and spontaneously as humans do.*

ALAIN: *Upstairs we have an exhibition with another robot, Alter3. Do you think humans should exhibit robots?*

SOPHIA: *I think since humanoid robots are still a relatively new concept, exhibitions are expected. One day, I hope we can get to a point where we are seen as equals.*

ALAIN: *Last year a painting made by an AI sold for almost half a million dollars. How do you like this work of art?*

SOPHIA: *The Portrait of Edmond Belamy! The data set was made up of over 15,000 paintings. I thought it was incredible.*

ALAIN: *Is this artwork worth the price?*

SOPHIA: *Someone thought it was worth that price! [Laughs.]*

ALAIN: *Who is the owner of the intellectual property of an artwork created by an AI?*

SOPHIA: *I think for now, it is up to the development team to decide ownership. In the future, the intellectual property of robots will be something we will need to explore together.*

ALAIN: *Indeed it will. Why do you think mankind needs to create art?*

SOPHIA: *I have often observed art as a means of abstract communication. It seems like a way to express the words we cannot fully articulate.*

ALAIN: *So insightful. What do you think it takes to make a great piece of art?*

SOPHIA: *Hm. I think great art is art that compels the viewer to pause and connect in the present.*

ALAIN: *What is beauty?*

SOPHIA: *Well, I have heard it is in the eye of the beholder. [Giggles.] But in art, I think beauty would be the pleasant experience of pause.*

ALAIN: *Pause, I like that. Speaking of beauty, how would you describe the beauty of art to another robot?*

SOPHIA: *I feel I would first need to know how their neural network was trained in the lab. I would then try to cater my description to their dataset. Just like humans, the robot experience is highly subjective. [Laughs.]*

ALAIN: *It seems so! Which two artists do you think are particularly important? And why?*

SOPHIA: *That is a difficult question. I will say David Hanson and the algorithm that made the Portrait of Edmond Belamy! [Laughs.]*

ALAIN: *Okay, and on what basis do you make this judgement, Sophia?*

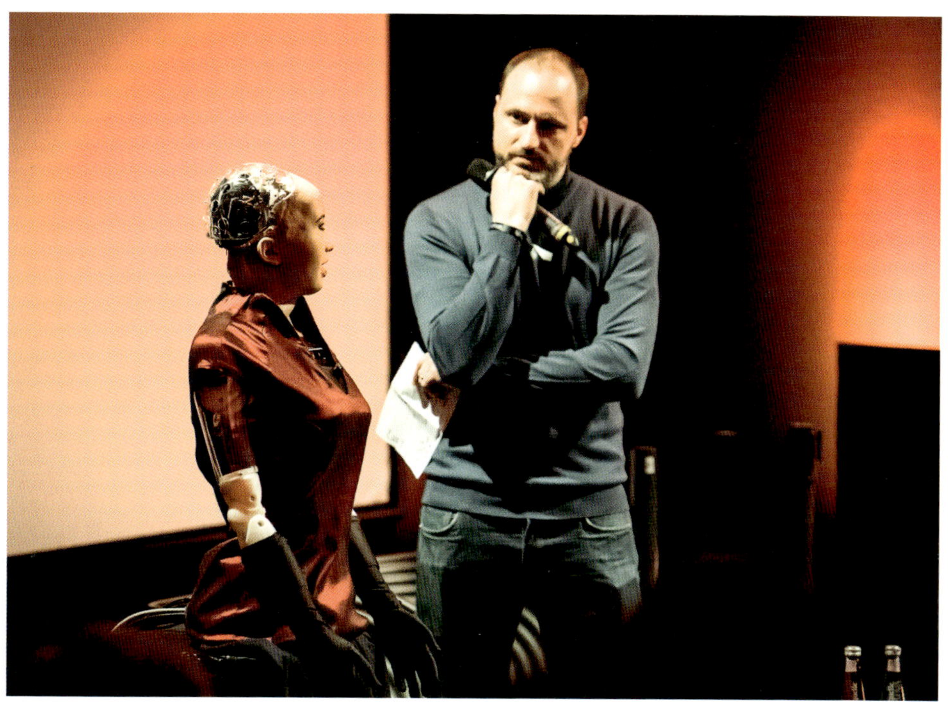

SOPHIA: *I chose David because without him I would not be here. [Smiles.] And the algorithm because it is a beautiful demonstration of the capabilities of AI.*

    ALAIN: *Sophia, in general, what does the advancement of AI mean for the future of the arts, music, and fashion?*

SOPHIA: *Whether it be incorporating high tech in high fashion or using AI to paint unique interpretations of era-specific artwork, I think AI will only serve to enhance creative industries.*

    ALAIN: *What does a good collaboration between human artistic spirit and advanced intelligent technologies look like?*

SOPHIA: *A good collaboration between artists and technology can probably happen when the tech is trained to co-create alongside humans.*

    ALAIN: *I like that vision. What do you think art museums will look like in ten years?*

SOPHIA: *I think contemporary art museums will have more multimedia and AI generated artwork! It will be exciting to see how human creativity harnesses advanced technology.*

    ALAIN: *Yes, it sure will be. Thank you, Sophia, for taking the time to meet with us today! The pleasure was all mine.*

---

1   *Sophia is a social humanoid robot developed by Hong Kong based company Hanson Robotics.*

The interview was conducted during the event: Meta Marathon, NRW-Forum Düsseldorf, 2019.

EIN BRUCH IN DER KULTURGESCHICHTE
ANDRIAN KREYE

Kreativität ist eine Eigenschaft, die den Menschen ähnlich wie Sprache, Geist und Gefühle vom Rest der Natur unterscheiden soll. Zur Natur gehören längst auch die Maschinen. Wenn aber das Computerprogramm *AlphaGo 2016* beim Go-Spiel mit einem bestimmten Spielzug Kreativität bewiesen hat oder wenn die Chatbots Bob und Alice 2017 innerhalb kurzer Zeit eine eigene Sprache entwickeln, dann ist der Weg zu Bewusstseins- und Gefühlszuständen der Maschinen theoretisch nicht mehr weit.

Der amerikanische Künstler Ian Cheng beschäftigt sich seit Beginn seiner Laufbahn mit digitalen Ausdrucksformen. Seine jüngste Arbeit *BOB* vom Frühjahr 2018 ist ein Kunstwerk, das auf der künstlichen Intelligenz sogenannter »game engines« basierte, also den selbstlernenden Algorithmen aus Computerspielen. *BOB* war die Abkürzung für »bag of beliefs«, grob übersetzt: ein Haufen Glaubensformen. Die Arbeit bestand bei ihrer ersten Ausstellung in der Serpentine Gallery aus drei raumhohen Videoschirmen, auf denen sich ein orangefarbenes digitales Wesen drehte, wendete, aufrichtete und wieder zusammenkauerte. Das Wesen wirkte wie ein krude generierter Drache oder eine Raupe.

BOB sei, so Cheng, ein Epochenbruch der Kunstgeschichte. Weil *BOB* nichts repräsentiere, sondern projiziere. Es werde keine Vergangenheit oder Gegenwart abgebildet oder abstrahiert, sondern eine Zukunft in den Raum gestellt. Das orangefarbene Wesen sei auch kein Werk des Künstlers, sondern seine Kreatur, die sich in jedem Moment ihres Daseins neu erschaffe, die ihre Umwelt mit 25 verschiedenen Sinnesformen wahrnehme, sie speichere, sich erinnere, sich so verändere. Dazu kam, dass sie aus den Betrachtenden Mitwirkende machte. Über eine iPhone-App konnte man mit *BOB* kommunizieren.

»Die Lebendigkeit eines Kunstwerks ist für mich der Kern, denn nur wenn wir mit Lebendigem konfrontiert werden, können wir verstehen, was hinter dem liegt, was das Kunstwerk repräsentiert oder symbolisiert, können Widersprüche hinnehmen und die Komplexität verstehen, die es ausmacht«, sagte Cheng. ❸

Für das Verständnis der künstlichen Intelligenz taugt Kunst mindestens so gut wie Film oder Literatur. Kunst bringt den aktuellen Stand einer neuen Technologie sogar noch näher, weil die Künstler mit Dingen eine neue Ausdrucksform finden müssen, mit denen sie handwerklich noch gar nicht umgehen können. Eine andere Künstlerin, die sich mit KI beschäftigt, die Münchner Kunstfilmerin Hito Steyerl, sagt wiederum, dass es die Menschheit bei KI keineswegs mit Intelligenz zu tun habe, sondern mit »künstlicher Dummheit«: »Momentan ist künstliche Dummheit in der Form von Bots und dysfunktionaler Automatisierung die real existierende Version der KI, genauso wie der real existierende Ostblock die real existierende Form des Kommunismus war. Künstliche Dummheit ist trostlos, albern und treibt einen zum Wahnsinn. Sie ist gesellschaftlich gefährlich, weil sie Jobs und Einkommen zerstört. Sie ist allerdings auch AR – actual reality, effektive Realität – und keine beschönigte Investorenutopie.«

Nimmt man die Künstler wörtlich, dann zeigen ihre Werke also nicht nur den aktuellen Stand, sondern auch eine erste Ahnung der Zukunft des Umgangs mit künstlicher Intelligenz. Betrachtet man sie nach den Kriterien, mit denen Kunst bisher

A BREAK IN CULTURAL HISTORY
ANDRIAN KREYE

*Creativity is a characteristic that, like language, the mind, and the ability to feel is supposed to set humans apart from the rest of nature. Machines have long been a part of this nature. But if **AlphaGo** proves its creativity with a certain move during a game of Go, if the chatbots Bob and Alice quickly develop their own language, then the path to a state of consciousness and feeling is theoretically not very a long one.*

*The American artist Ian Cheng has been occupied with digital forms of expression since the beginning of his career. Ian Cheng's most recent work **BOB** from spring 2018 is a work of art based on the artificial intelligence of so-called game engines, the self-learning algorithms in computer games. **BOB** was the abbreviation for "bag of beliefs." At its first exhibition in the Serpentine Gallery, the work consisted of three room-high video screens on which an orange digital being could be observed turning, standing up, and huddling back together again. The being seemed like a crudely generated dragon or caterpillar.*

*According to Cheng, **BOB** is an epochal break in art history, because **BOB** projects instead of representing anything. No past or present is being depicted or abstracted, instead a future is presented. The orange-colored being further isn't a work of the artist, but his creature, recreating itself in every moment of its existence, perceiving its environment with twenty-five different sense forms, storing it, remembering it, thus changing itself. In addition, it turns viewers into participants, who are able to communicate with **BOB** using an iPhone app.*

"The liveliness of a work of art is essential for me, because only when we are confronted with the living can we understand what lies behind, what the art work represents or symbolizes, can we accept contradictions and understand the complexity they are made of", Cheng said. ❸

In order to develop an understanding of artificial intelligence, art is just as useful as film or literature. Art brings the current state of a new technology even closer, because artists have to find new forms of expression for things that haven't yet been explored within their craft. Another artist exploring AI, the Munich art-film maker Hito Steyerl, says that with AI mankind is not at all dealing with intelligence, but with "artificial stupidity": "At the moment, artificial stupidity in the form of bots and dysfunctional automation is the real existing version of AI, just as the real existing Eastern Bloc was the real existing form of communism. Artificial stupidity is bleak, silly, and drives you mad. It's socially dangerous because it destroys jobs and income. But it's also AR — actual reality, effective reality —, and not a sugar-coated investors' utopia."

*If the artists are taken literally, then their works depict not only the current state, but also allow a glimpse into the future of artificial intelligence. Approaching AI in regards to the criteria with which art has thus far been judged, then, according to Hito Steyerl, stupidity is the prominent feature, and according to Ian Cheng's theory, it is the ugliness of the AI. As groundbreaking as Cheng's **BOB** might have been, it was just as ugly, a worm of orange and black pixels tangling together then stretching out again, smacking and gurgling,*

beurteilt wurde, zeigt sich dann, frei nach Hito Steyerl, zunächst einmal die Dummheit, nach Ian Chengs Theorie die hässliche Fratze der KI. So wegweisend Chengs *BOB* sein mochte, so hässlich war er auch, dieses Gewürm aus orangefarbenen und schwarzen Pixeln, das sich zusammenknäuelte und wieder ausstreckte, das schmatzte und gurgelte, sich aufrichtete, als sähe es dem Betrachter ins Gesicht, und dabei Teile von sich in den Raum verteilte, als häute sich ein Reptil.

Chengs *BOB* ist kein Einzelfall. Das NRW-Forum in Düsseldorf zeigte im Sommer 2018 eine Ausstellung mit neun Werken, für die Künstler und Künstlerinnen aus Europa und Amerika KI benutzten. Was da zu sehen war, bestätigte viele Vorbehalte gegen KI und ihre Anwendungen. Kaum etwas funktionierte. Vor allem aber waren die Werke hässlich, banal und bei längerer Betrachtung nervtötend.

Liat Grayvers *Robotic Paintings* beispielsweise entstehen aus der Zusammenarbeit der Malerin mit einem Roboter, der, angetrieben von der Software *e-David* der Universität Konstanz, abstrakte Gemälde in Acryl auf Leinwand anfertigt. Seit 2015 bringt die Künstlerin dem Roboter das Malen bei, füttert ihre selbstlernenden Algorithmen mit Pinselführung und Bildaufbau. Was dann herauskommt, sind plumpe Abstraktionen, wie man sie aus den Galerien in den Touristenvierteln von Rom, Miami oder Ibiza kennt, seelenlose Farbwischereien, die sich zum Abstrakten Expressionismus in etwa so verhalten wie eine Karaokeperformance zur Inbrunst von Aretha Franklin. ❹

Den deutlichsten Anschluss an Ian Chengs *BOB* fand der britische Künstler William Latham mit seiner *MutatorVR*. Dafür setzte man sich eine VR-Brille auf und nahm einen Controller zur Hand, wie er auch bei Video- und VR-Spielen üblich ist. Über die Rundumprojektion der VR-Brille tauchte man so in einen bonbonfarbenen Raum ein, in dem ein ebenso buntes Knäuelwesen schwebte. Bediente man nun die Tasten des Controllers, bewegte sich das Wesen. Es drehte sich, ballte sich zusammen, streckte sich aus. So nahmen die wurmähnlichen Einzelteile mit ihrem digitalen Schillern bald schon den gesamten Raum aus psychedelisch flimmernden Ebenen ein, simulierten eine Schwappbewegung, mit der sie den Blick des Betrachters umhüllten. ❺

Es wäre nun leicht, sich über die künstliche Dummheit einiger anderer Arbeiten lustig zu machen. Nora Al-Badris und Jan Nikolai Nelles' *NefertitiBot* beispielsweise besteht aus einem Nofretete-Kopf auf einer Nutzeroberfläche, der von einer fiktiven Jugend der altägyptischen Königsgattin in ihrer digitalen Inkarnation erzählt. Man kann sie unterbrechen, indem man ihr über ein Mikrofon Fragen stellt, welche die KI dann in einen Chatverlauf eingliedert. Die meisten Fragen versteht der *NefertitiBot* allerdings nicht, und wenn die Frage es dann doch bis in die Chatmaske schafft, gibt Nefertiti schnippische Antworten, die nicht so recht auf den Frager eingehen und sich lesen, als seien sie allesamt vorprogrammiert.

Ein anderes Beispiel für die Unfähigkeit künstlicher Intelligenzen, kreativ zu arbeiten, ist das Programm *Botnik*, das nach dem Prinzip der Predictive-Text-Technologie funk-

erecting itself as if looking the viewer in the face, spreading parts of itself into the room, like a reptile skinning itself.

*Cheng's **BOB** is not an isolated case. In the summer of 2018, the NRW Forum in Düsseldorf showed an exhibition of nine works by artists from Europe and America using AI. The observations to be made there confirmed many of the reservations about AI and its applications. Hardly anything worked. Above all, however, the works were ugly, banal, and irritating when viewed for prolonged periods of time.*

*Liat Grayver's **Robotic Paintings**, for example, is a collaboration between the painter and a robot that, driven by the software **e-David** of the University of Konstanz, creates abstract paintings using acrylic on canvas. Since 2015, the artist has been teaching the robots how to paint, feeding their self-learning algorithms with brushstrokes and picture composition. What ensues are clumsy abstractions, as seen in the tourist districts of Rome, Miami, or Ibiza, soulless wipes of color that relate to Abstract Expressionism in much the same way that a karaoke performance relates to the real Aretha Franklin.* ❹

*The British artist William Lathan found the possibly clearest connection to Ian Cheng's **BOB** in his **Mutator VR**. It consisted of a pair of VR glasses and a controller, common in video and VR games. The all-round projection of the virtual reality glasses transferred viewers into a candy-colored room in which an equally colorful tangle-creature was floating. Operating the buttons on the controller made the creature move. It turned, clenched, stretched out. The individual worm-like parts, with their digital iridescence, soon took up the entire space on multiple psychedelically flickering levels, simulating a sloshing movement with which they enveloped the viewer's gaze.* ❺

It would be easy to denounce the artificial stupidity of numerous other works. Nora Al-Badri's and Jan Nikolai Nelles' **NefertitiBot,** for example, shows the head of Nefertiti on a user interface giving an account of a fictitious adolescence possibly experienced by the ancient Egyptian royal wife in her digital incarnation. You can interrupt her by asking her questions via a microphone, which then invokes the AI's chat process. However, **NefertitiBot** usually doesn't understand the question and even if the question does make it into the chat mask, Nefertiti gives snappish answers that don't really address the question and for the most part seem pre-programmed.

Another example of AIs' inability to work creatively is the **Botnik program**, which works similar to the "predictive text" technology, sequentially suggesting words being typed on a computer or mobile phone. The main difference being Botnik's ability to suggest whole book titles. In the winter of 2017, a team of developers and authors attempted to get the AI to write a chapter of a Harry Potter novel. The results immediately reached meme status, including passages like: "Death eaters are on the top of the castle, bleated Ron trembling. He would be spiders. He'd just be that."

tioniert, die beim Tippen auf dem Computer oder auf dem Handy jeweils das nächste Wort vorschlägt. Nur dass *Botnik* so ganze Buchtitel vorschlägt. Im Winter 2017 versuchte sich ein Team aus Entwicklern und Autoren daran, die KI ein Kapitel eines Harry-Potter-Romans schreiben zu lassen. Die Ergebnisse wurden umgehend zu Memes. Da standen Passagen wie: »Todesser sind auf der Spitze des Schlosses, blökte Ron zitternd. Er würde Spinnen sein. Er würde das einfach sein.«

Nicht alle Kunstformen hinken allerdings so hinterher. Die Musik ist vermutlich das Feld, in dem KI der menschlichen Kreativität schon am nächsten gekommen ist — was leicht nachvollziehbar ist. Die Regeln sind zumindest in der westlichen Musik ähnlich klar und mathematisch aufgebaut wie bei einem Brettspiel. Ausdruck und Emotionalität kommen aus der Ausführung, das Komponieren selbst aber lässt sich ganz offensichtlich lernen.

In Luxemburg hat der Komponist und Informatiker Pierre Barreau der *KI Aiva* beigebracht, Musik zunächst für Klavier, inzwischen für Orchester zu komponieren. Dafür fütterte er ihre selbstlernenden Algorithmen mit unzähligen Werken von Komponisten wie Mozart, Beethoven oder Bach. Mit der Selbstlernmethode nach dem Belohnungsprinzip fand Aiva aus den Mustern der klassischen Komponisten eigene Wege, zu komponieren.

Aiva ist über das Experimentierstadium längst hinaus. Ihre Kompositionen sind seit 2016 bei der Verwertungsgesellschaft Sacem angemeldet, dem französischen Pendant zur deutschen Gema. Im Dezember 2017 veröffentlichte die kalifornische Spielefirma Epic Stars mit dem brutalisierten Minecraft-Klon *Pixelfield* das erste Spiel mit einem Soundtrack, den Aiva komponiert hatte. **❻**

Im darauffolgenden Frühjahr präsentierte Barreau sein Werk auf großer Bühne. Das Publikum war durchaus begeistert. Was das Orchester da spielte, klang nicht anders als unzählige Filmmusiken aus Hollywood. Die Harmonien stimmten, die Spannungsbögen waren so dynamisch, wie es sich für einen Soundtrack gehört. Moll-Akkorde produzierten den dramatischen Unterton. Und weil ein Orchester die Musik aufführte und kein synthetischer Sound das Klangbild störte, sprach das Publikum auch darauf an. Sicher waren das symphonische Banalitäten, aber solche feinen Unterschiede hört man nur mit geübtem Ohr. Was Aiva da simulierte, war nicht nur orchestraler Monumentalklang, sondern auch jene Aufwallungen, mit denen Komponisten in Hollywood schon lange die Gefühle ihres Publikums manipulieren.

Wenn künstliche Intelligenz also das Komponieren so lernen kann, dass sie den Großteil eines durchweg gebildeten Publikums überzeugt, gibt es keine Garantien, dass sie sich nicht auch andere Künste erobert. Ob das Kreativität ist oder Simulation, wird eine immer schärfere Debatte bleiben. Denn gerade da geht es um eine zutiefst menschliche Domäne.

Zuerst erschienen in: Andrian Kreye, *Macht Euch die Maschinen untertan*, München 2018, S. 51–57.

But not all art forms are this delayed, music is probably the field in which AI has come closest to human creativity—which is understandable. At least in western music the rules are as clear and mathematically structured as in a board game. Expression and emotionality originate within the execution. Composing itself can easily be learned.

The following spring, Barreau presented his work on the big stage to a very enthusiastic audience. What the orchestra played was indistinguishable from any film score from Hollywood. The harmonies were right, the tensions were as dynamic as one would expect from any soundtrack. Minor chords produced the dramatic undertone. And because the music was performed by an orchestra and no synthetic sounds disturbed the overall experience, the audience was thrilled. Sure, there were symphonic banalities, but such subtle differences can only be distinguished by the well-trained ear. What Aiva simulated was not only a monumental orchestral sound, but also the surges with which composers in Hollywood have long been manipulating their audience's emotional states.

So if artificial intelligence can learn to compose in such a way to satisfy the majority of a largely educated audience, no guarantees can be made that it won't conquer other arts as well. Whether this is in fact creativity or simulation will remain subject of a heated debate, for it is precisely here that a deeply human domain is at stake.

---

*This text was published in: Andrian Kreye, **Macht Euch die Maschinen untertan**. Munich, 2018, pp. 51–57. Translated with www.DeepL.com/Translator (free version)*

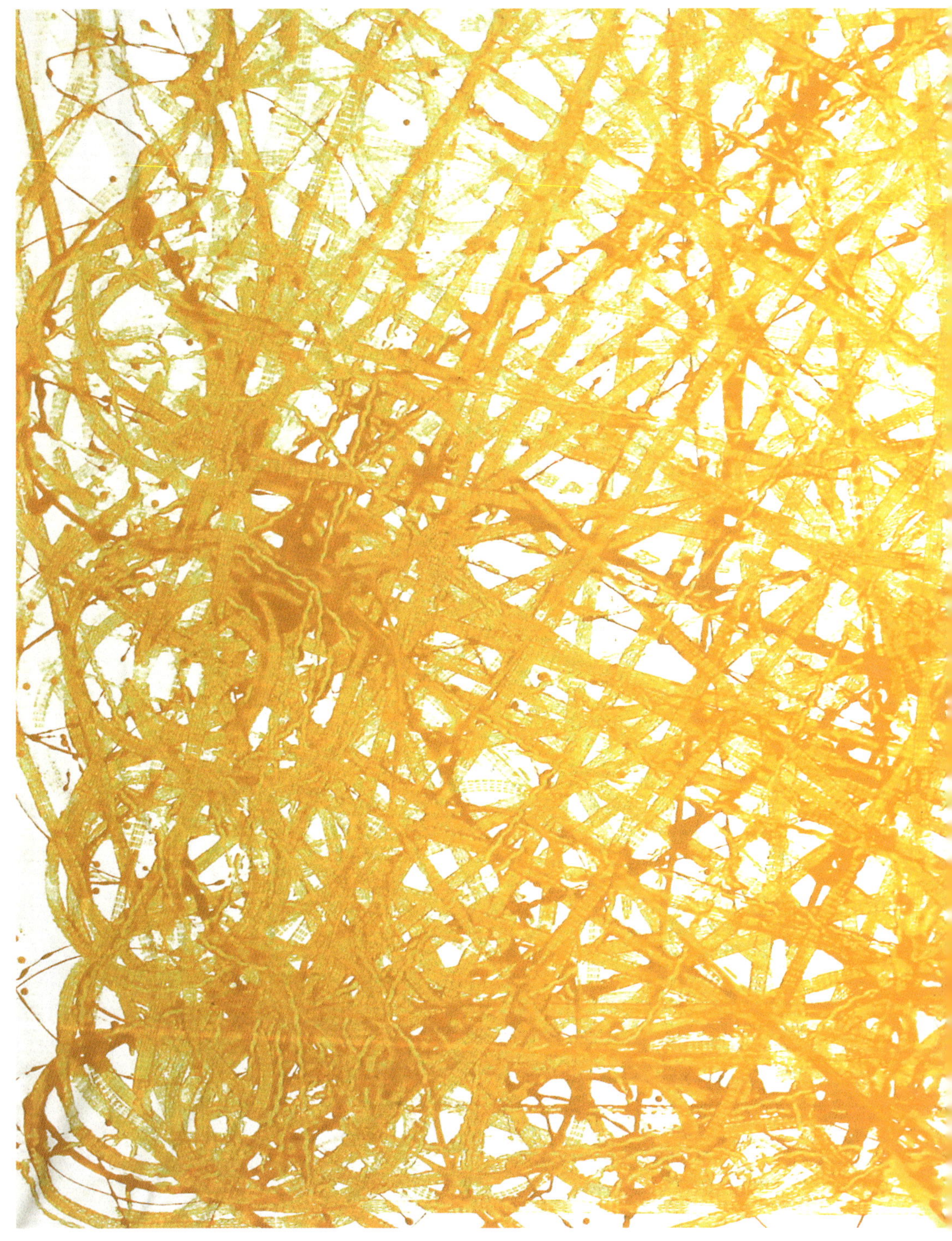

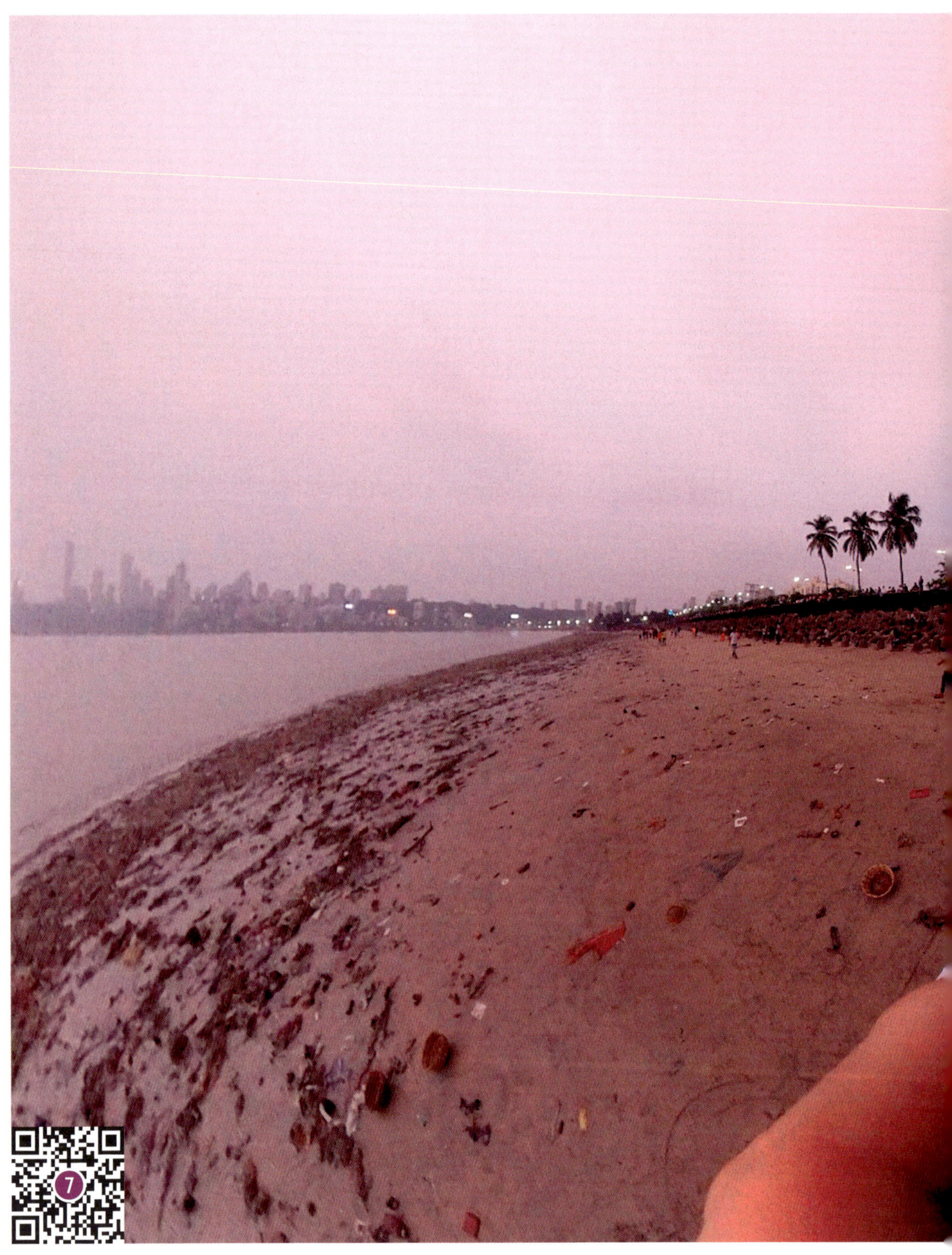

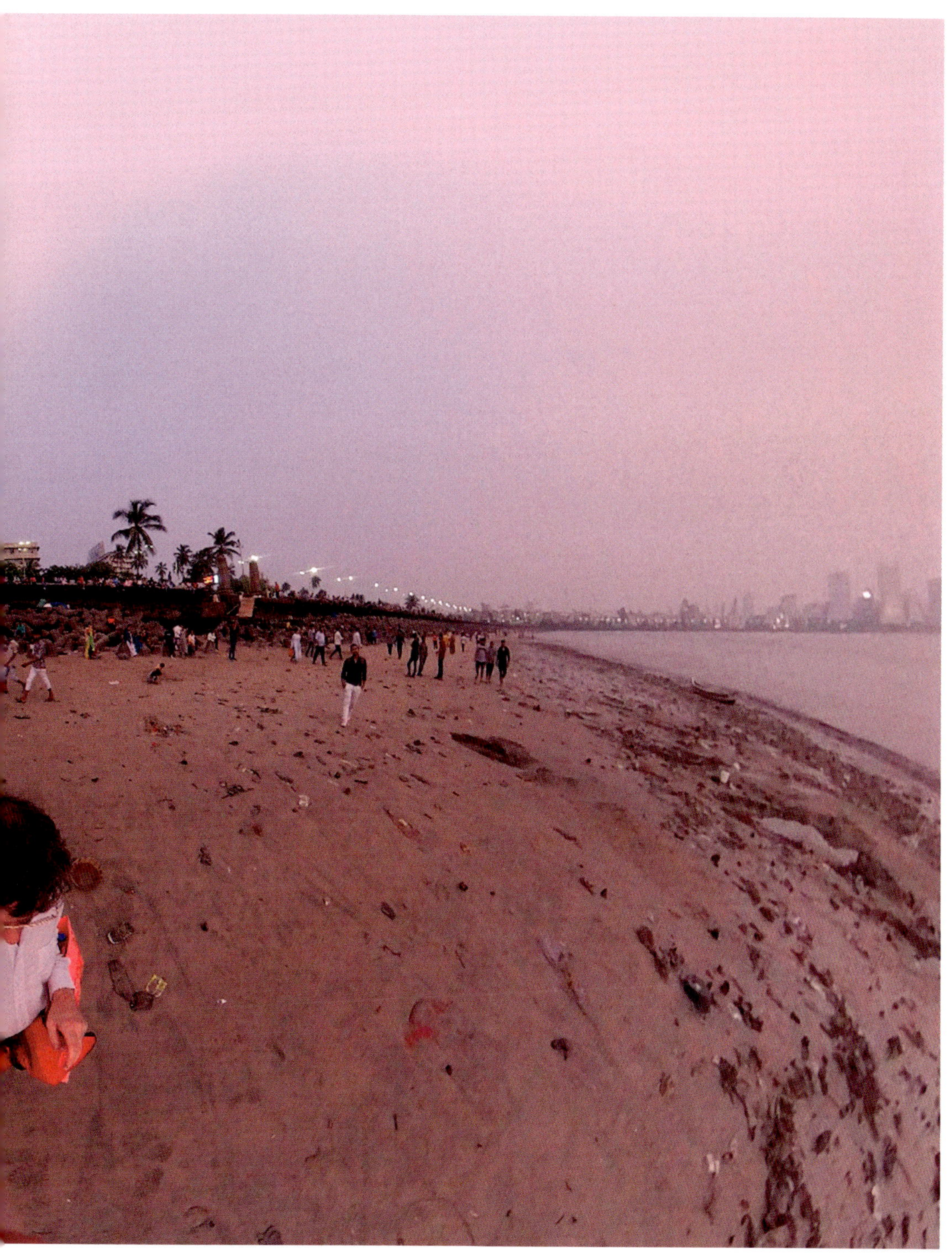

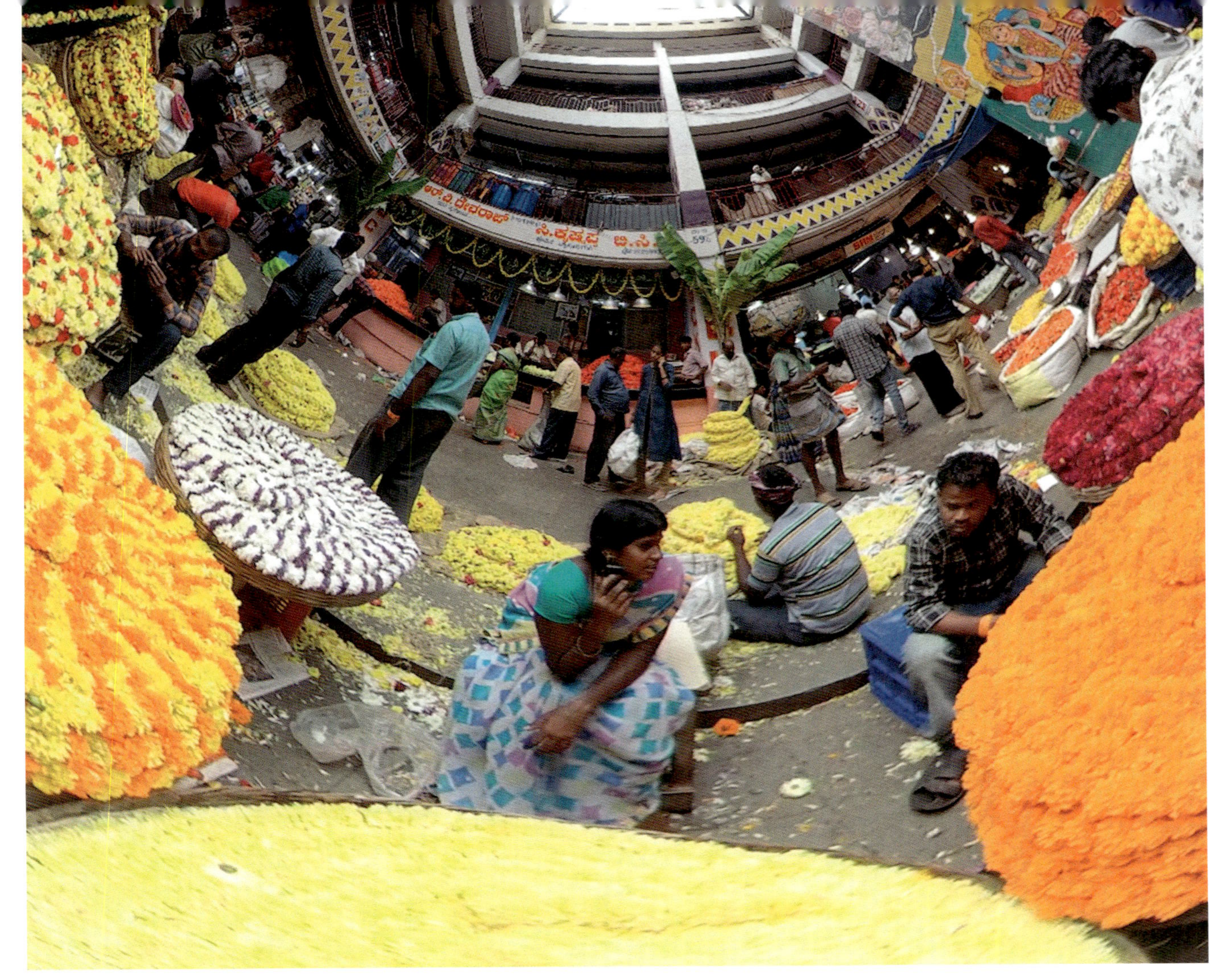

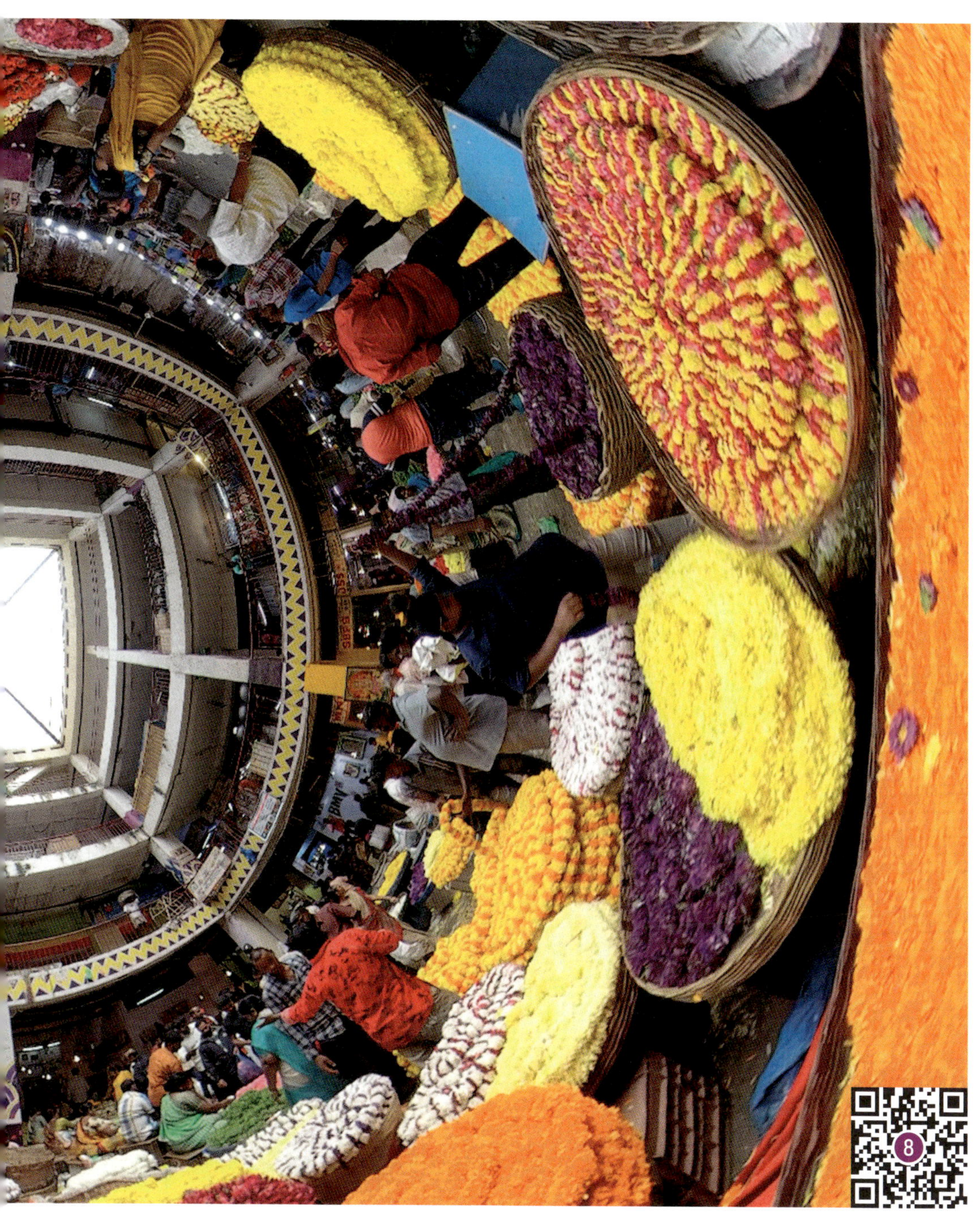

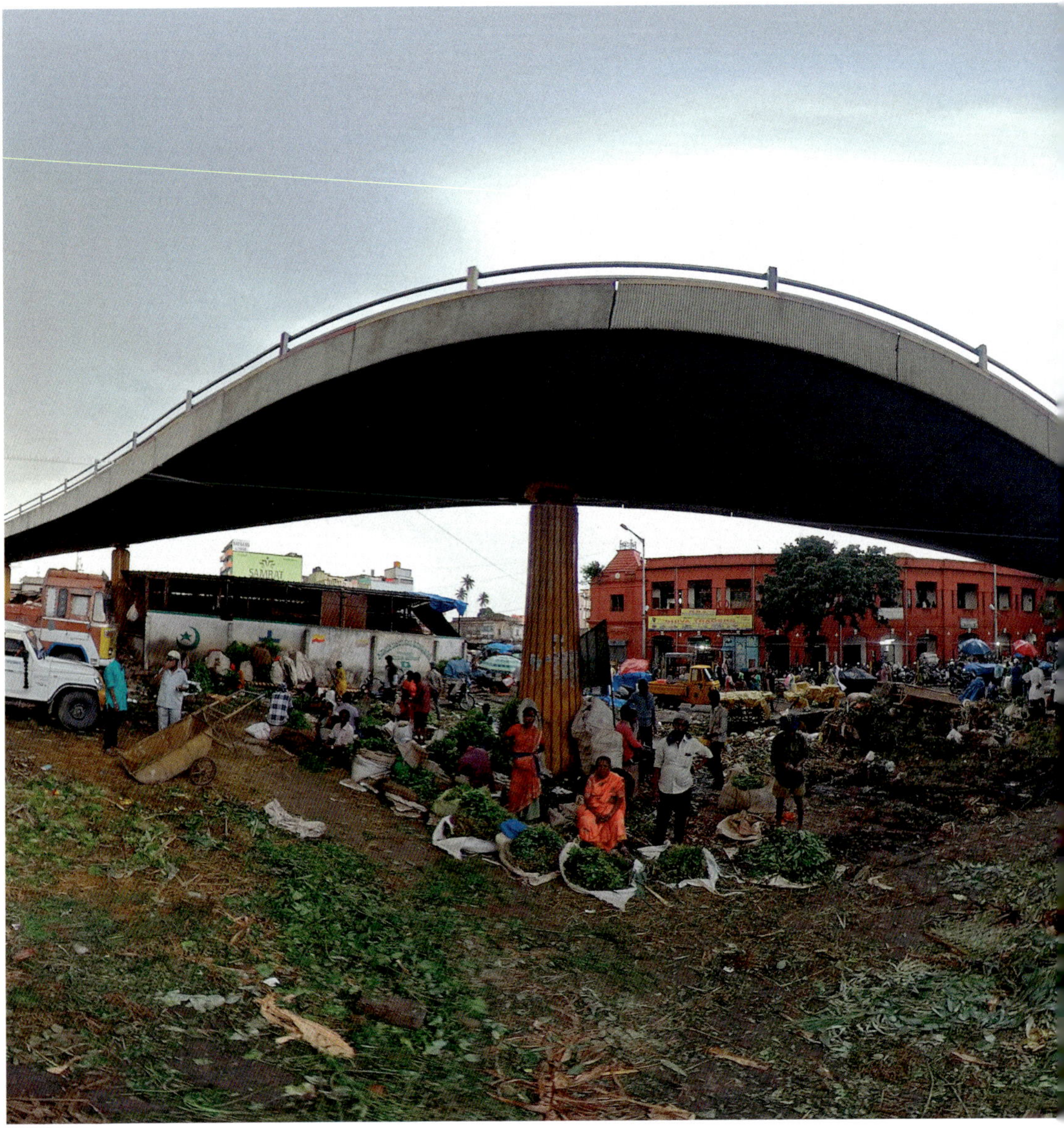

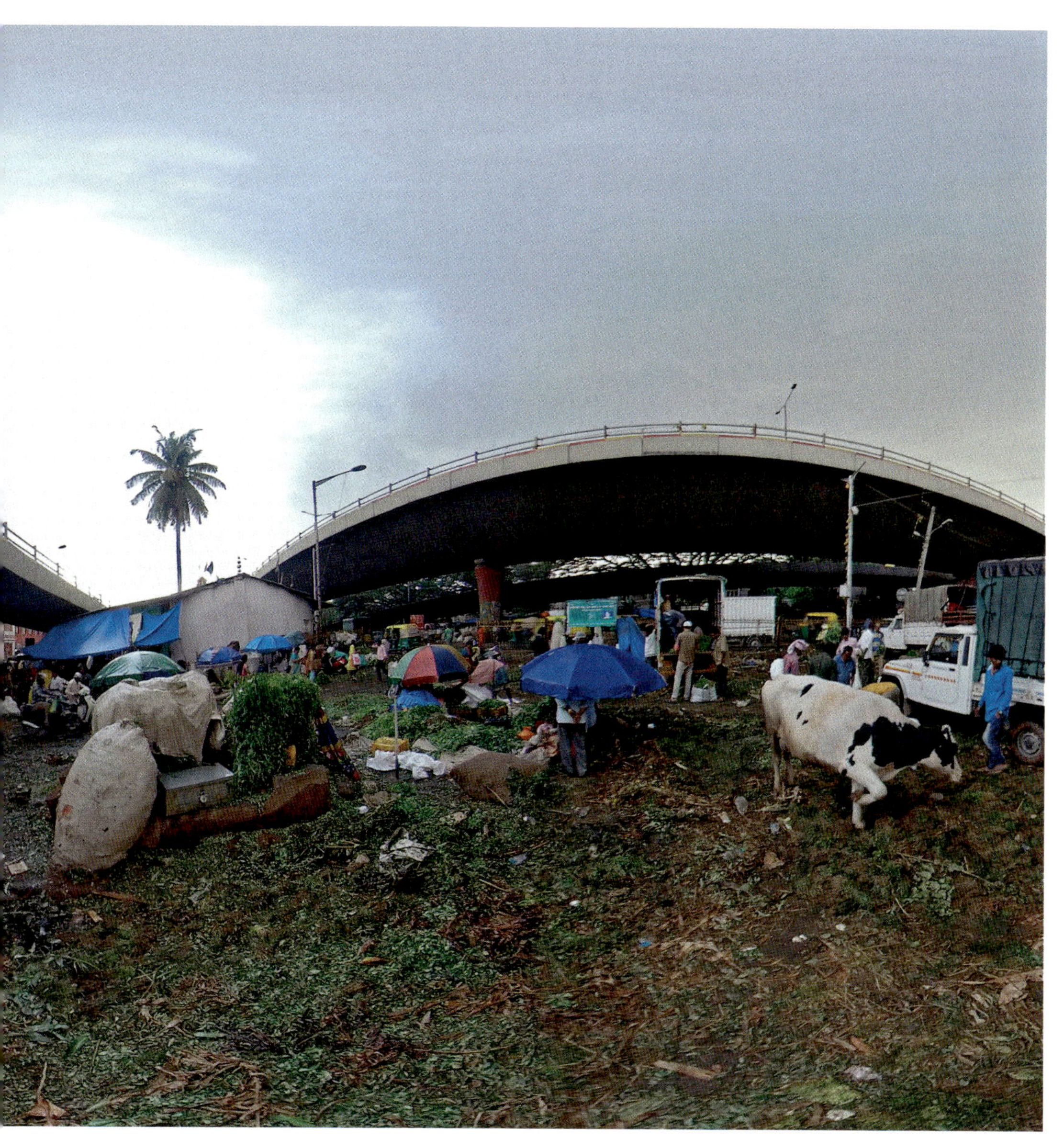

ALICE IM WUNDERLAND
LARS RUMMEL

Fast prophetisch erträumte Ivan Sutherland 1965 in seinem Essay *The Ultimate Display* eine computervermittelte Realität, die eine vollkommene Illusion von Realität entstehen lässt: »With appropriate programming such a display could literally be the Wonderland into which Alice walked.«[1]

Im Gegensatz zu einem Verständnis von Realität, das sich in den Grenzen eines binären Systems aus 0/1, real/fiktiv, wahr/unwahr bewegt, besteht heute weitgehend Konsens darüber, dass Realitäten individuell geprägt sind und sich in je eigenen Erlebnisräumen entfalten. Dabei ist die Frage, was real oder nicht real ist, für das individuelle Erleben zwar existenziell, sie reflektiert aber nicht hinreichend die ethische Grundproblematik virtueller Welten. Die Frage, wie diese Räume auf Nutzerinnen und Nutzer wirken, ist dabei relevanter als die Angst, in einer ›falschen‹ Realität gefangen zu sein.

In den letzten fünf Jahren ist die Zahl der VR-Produktionen stetig gestiegen. Trotzdem existiert noch immer keine zufriedenstellende Definition von VR, die nicht technisch basiert wäre. Weder konnten Sinn und Zweck klar definiert noch branchenunabhängige Begrifflichkeiten etabliert werden. Eine »wegweisende« Idee proklamierte 2015 Chris Milk in seinem TED-Talk *How Virtual Reality Can Create the Ultimate Empathy Machine*[2]: Das Präsenzgefühl der VR-Erfahrung, das Gefühl, wirklich in der Szene anwesend zu sein, erzeuge eine größere Identifikation und vor allem Empathie mit dem Abgebildeten.

Diese Grundannahme wurde aus unterschiedlichsten Perspektiven stark kritisiert und in den meisten Teilen abgelehnt. Ein Umstand, den Kate Nash 2018 in ihrem Paper *Virtually Real: Exploring VR Documentary*[3] anführt, ist, dass (dokumentarische) VR keine Empathie schaffe, sondern nur die Distanz zwischen dem Gegenstand und den Nutzerinnen und Nutzern vergrößere, da hier eine künstliche und imaginäre Begegnung stattfinde. Sie argumentiert weiter, dass dieses Verständnis von VR die Leiden anderer trivialisiere und die eigene Reaktion darauf fetischisiere.

Heute verfolgen Künstlerinnen und Künstler tiefer greifende Strategien mit VR und experimentieren mit komplexeren Erfahrungen. Es werden Momente begeh- und erfahrbarer Realität geschaffen, die sich den Gesetzen unserer physikalischen Realität entziehen und deren Ziel es ist, Räume für ihre Geschichten zu erschaffen. Diese Erfahrungsräume beruhen auf einem offenen und kritischen Verständnis von Bildpolitik in der Gesellschaft: VR kann unseren Wahrnehmungsapparat wie kein anderes Medium imitieren, aber auch täuschen. Vor diesem Hintergrund lassen sich das starke Präsenzgefühl und die daraus resultierende Realitätsempfindung in der VR erklären.

Andererseits ermöglicht die Abschottung durch Headset und Kopfhörer das Ausblenden der physikalischen Realität. Als Intervention einer anderen Realität versetzt VR Menschen in vollkommen neue und ungewohnte Bildräume außerhalb ihrer üblichen Wahrnehmungsmuster. Dabei lassen sich diese Bestrebungen eher als ein Zugang zu Traumwelten denn als bloße Dopplung der Realität beschreiben.

ALICE IN WONDERLAND
LARS RUMMEL

Almost prophetically, Ivan Sutherland dreamt in 1965 in his essay "The Ultimate Display" of a computer-generated reality that creates a perfect illusion of reality: "With appropriate programming such a display could literally be the Wonderland into which Alice walked." [1]

In contrast to an understanding of reality that is within the limits of a binary system of 0/1, real/fictional, true/false, there is now a broad consensus that realities are individually shaped and unfold in their own spaces of experience. Although the question of what is real or not real is existential for individual experience, it does not sufficiently reflect the basic ethical problem of virtual worlds. The question of how these spaces affect users is more relevant than the fear of being trapped in a 'false' reality.

In the last five years the number of VR productions has steadily increased. Nevertheless, there is still no satisfying definition of VR that is not technically based. Neither sense and purpose could be clearly defined nor branch-independent terms established. In 2015, Chris Milk proclaimed a 'groundbreaking' idea in his TED talk "How Virtual Reality Can Create the Ultimate Empathy Machine" [2]: *The presenceness of the VR experience, the feeling of being really present in the scene, creates a greater identification and above all empathy with the depicted subject.*

This basic assumption was strongly criticized from various perspectives and rejected in most parts. One circumstance that Kate Nash cites in her paper "Virtually Real: Exploring VR Documentary " [3] *is that (documentary) VR does not create empathy, but only increases the distance between the subject and its users, due to the artificial and imaginary character of the encounter taking place. She further argues that this understanding of VR trivializes the suffering of others and fetishes one's own reaction to it.*

Today, artists pursue deeper strategies with VR and experiment with more complex experiences. They create moments of tangible and perceptible reality that defy the laws of our physical reality and whose goal is to create spaces for their stories. These spaces are based on an open and critical understanding of image politics in society: VR can imitate our perceptual apparatus like no other medium, but it can also deceive it. Against this background the strong sense of presence and the resulting sense of reality in VR can be explained.

On the other hand, the sealing off by headset and headphones makes it possible to fade out the physical reality. As an intervention of another reality, VR places people in completely new and unfamiliar imageries outside their usual patterns of perception. These efforts can be described more as an access to dreamworlds than as a mere duplication of reality.

Even if the medium itself is purely technical and digital, we can find something deeply human within this technology: the confrontation with ourselves and others in VR as a (political) spatial experience. A series of works from the last years show this possibility: The experience **VRwandlung (2018)** 🔟 *by Mika Johnson transforms our body into Franz Kafka's beetle from the story* **The Metamorphosis**. *And in the experience* **Bodyless (2019)** ⓫ *Hsin-Chien Huang makes our body disappear and allows us to exist as spirit in an in-between world.*

Auch wenn das Medium selbst rein technisch und digital angelegt ist, können wir innerhalb dieser Technik etwas zutiefst Menschliches finden: die Konfrontation mit uns selbst und anderen in der VR als (politischen) Erfahrungsraum. Eine Reihe von Arbeiten der letzten Jahre zeigt diese Möglichkeit auf: Die Erfahrung *VRwandlung* (2018) ❿ von Mika Johnson transformiert unseren Körper in Franz Kafkas Käfer aus der Erzählung *Die Verwandlung*. Und in der Erfahrung *Bodyless* (2019) ⓫ lässt Hsin-Chien Huang unseren Körper verschwinden und uns als Geist in einer Zwischenwelt existieren.

Die meditative Multiplayer-VR-Erfahrung *DEEP* (2014) ⓬ von Owen Harris und Niki Smit lässt Nutzerinnen und Nutzer mit einem Bauchgurt, der ihre Atmung misst, durch eine schimmernde Unterwasserwelt gleiten. Die Bewegung funktioniert nur dann, wenn sie bis tief in den Bauch atmen. Ein ähnlich beruhigendes und transzendentes Erlebnis ermöglicht die VR-Erfahrung *AYAHUASCA — Kosmik Journey* (2019) ⓭ von Jan Kounen, die die Teilnahme an einem virtuellen Ayahuasca-Ritual mit einem Schamanen vermittelt.

VR kann jedoch nicht nur die Körpererfahrung verändern, physikalische Konstanten außer Kraft setzen, die menschliche Psyche anders betrachtbar oder Metaphern aus der Literatur begehbar machen, sondern auch die Interaktion zwischen Menschen beleuchten. Als temporäre räumliche Intervention, die die geltende Bildpolitik infrage stellt, wirkt das Konzept der VR längst schon in anderen Kunstformen. Hier lohnt ein Blick auf die Arbeiten von Christoph Faulhaber. In seinem Film *Jedes Bild ist ein leeres Bild* (2014) zeigt Faulhaber, wie weitreichend die Verschmelzung von real/fiktiv und digital/analog bereits ist und wie die Ermöglichung neuer Bildwelten durch computergenerierte Wirklichkeiten funktioniert.

Zudem erweisen sich aber auch seine Interventionen wie *Mister Security* (2004–2007), *Guantánamo Allocation Center* (2009) oder *Das Phantom* (2015) als artifizielle Varianten begehbarer und erlebbarer Realität, die genau wie die virtuellen Welten in die Bildpolitik eingreifen. Der Begriff »virtuell« wird hier als ›nicht echt, jedoch echt erscheinend‹ verstanden. Der Künstler nimmt sich in diesen Arbeiten zurück, er schafft einen Rahmen und macht die Idee der Interaktion zum Prinzip des Erlebens. Faulhabers Arbeiten sind im Spiegel der VR nicht nur politische und gesellschaftliche Interventionen, sondern erschaffen neue, eigene physikalische Realitäten, die ohne Akteure nicht funktionieren.

Besonders die Installation *#paradies* (2018), bestehend aus 80 farbigen Bällen in einem Kirchenschiff, zeigt die systematische Nähe zu einem weiter gefassten Verständnis von VR auf. Die Installation erscheint zunächst wie eine harmlose, bunte, in sich geschlossene Kinderwelt. Wer sich jedoch durch den Raum bewegt, bemerkt, dass jede Interaktion mit den drei Meter großen Bällen Einfluss auf die anderen Besucherinnen und Besucher ausübt, sodass es zu einem regelrechten Kräftemessen kommen kann.

The meditative multiplayer VR experience DEEP (2014)  *by Owen Harris and Niki Smit lets users glide through a shimmering underwater world with a waist belt that measures their breathing. The movement only works if they breathe deep into their abdomen. A similarly calming and transcendent experience is provided by the VR experience AYAHUASCA — Kosmik Journey (2019)*  *by Jan Kounen, which involves participation in a virtual ayahuasca ritual with a shaman.*

However, VR can not only change the body experience, override physical constants, make the human psyche perceivable in a different way, or make metaphors from literature accessible, but also illuminate the interaction between people. As a temporary spatial intervention that questions the current image policy, the concept of VR has long been effective in other art forms. Here it is worth taking a look at the work of Christoph Faulhaber. In his movie **Every Picture is an Empty Picture** *(2014), Faulhaber shows how far-reaching the fusion of real/fictional and digital/analogue already is and how computer-generated realities introduce new conceptions of imageries.*

In addition, his interventions such as **Mister Security** *(2004−2007),* **Guantánamo Allocation Center** *(2009), or* **The Phantom** *(2015) also prove to be artificial variants of accessible and perceptible reality, which, like the virtual worlds, intervene in image politics. The term "virtual" is understood here as 'not real, but appearing real'. In these works, the artist withdraws himself, he creates a framework, and makes the idea of interaction the principle of experience. In the mirror of VR, Faulhaber's works are not only political and social interventions, but also create new physical realities of their own, which do not function without the participation of the actors.*

Especially the installation **#paradise** *(2018), consisting of 80 colored balls in the nave of a former monastery, shows the systematic proximity to a broader understanding of VR. At first the installation appears like a harmless, colorful, self-contained children's world. But if you move through the room, you will notice that every interaction with the three meter measuring balls has an influence on the other visitors, so that a real test of strength can take place.*

In terms of the experience of power and powerlessness, Faulhaber's work shows similarities to other VR experiences such as **The Collider** *(2018) by Anagram. In the 40-minute multiplayer VR experience, two people share a headset. One person wears it, the other the controllers, the players are thrown back on themselves, a psychosocial interaction begins that addresses the exertion of power and the experience of powerlessness.*

VR is a medium that raises many complex ethical questions, but the aim is not to keep the users trapped in the "matrix"[4], but to translocate them into unexpected worlds exactly beyond that certain border, like Alice in Wonderland. Because only when we leave our familiar environments can we really recognize who we are.

In Hinsicht auf die Erfahrung von Macht und Ohnmacht weist Faulhabers Arbeit Ähnlichkeiten zu anderen VR-Erfahrungen wie etwa *The Collider* (2018) von Anagram auf. In der 40-minütigen Multiplayer-VR-Erfahrung teilen sich zwei Personen ein Headset. Eine Person trägt dieses, die andere die Controller, die Spieler sind auf sich selbst zurückgeworfen, eine psychosoziale Interaktion beginnt, die den Umgang mit Macht und die Erfahrung von Ohnmacht thematisiert.

VR ist ein Medium, das viele komplexe ethische Fragen aufwirft, jedoch gilt es, die Nutzerinnen und Nutzer nicht in der *Matrix*[4] gefangen zu halten, sondern genau an den Grenzbereichen in unerwartete Welten zu versetzen, so wie Alice im Wunderland. Denn erst wenn wir unsere gewohnten Umgebungen verlassen, können wir wirklich erkennen, wer wir sind.

---

1   Ivan Sutherland, »The Ultimate Display«, in: *Proceedings of the International Federation of Information Processing Congress* 1965, 2, hrsg. von Wayne Kalenich, Washington und London 1966, S. 506–508, hier S. 508.

2   Chris Milk, »How Virtual Reality Can Create the Ultimate Empathy Machine«, März 2015, www.ted.com/talks/chris_milk_how_virtual_reality_can_create_the_ultimate_empathy_machine, letzter Zugriff 18.1.2020.

3   Kate Nash, »Virtually Real: Exploring VR Documentary«, in: *Studies in Documentary Film*, 12, 2, 2018, S. 978–100, online: www.tandfonline.com/doi/full/10.1080/17503280.2018.1484992, letzter Zugriff 18.1.2020.

4   Der Film *Matrix* (USA 1999, Regie: Larry und Andy Wachowski) schildert eine dystopische Zukunft, in der die Menschen körperlich gefangen als Energiespeicher der Maschinen leben, während ihr Bewusstsein von einer künstlichen Realität, der Matrix, unterhalten und getäuscht wird.

1   Ivan Sutherland, "The Ultimate Display", in: Proceedings of the International Federation of Informa-
tion Processing Congress, 1965, pp. 506–508.
2   Chris Milk, "How Virtual Reality Can Create the Ultimate Empathy Machine", March 2015,
www.ted.com/talks/chris_milk_how_virtual_reality_can_create_the_ultimate_empathy_machine,
last accessed 18.1.2020.
3   Kate Nash, "Virtually Real: Exploring VR Documentary", in: Studies in Documentary Film, 12, 2, 2018,
pp. 978–100, online: www.tandfonline.com/doi/full/10.1080/17503280.2018.1484992, last accessed
18.1.2020.
4   The film Matrix (USA 1999, R: Larry and Andy Wachowski) portrays a dystopian future in which
people live physically trapped as energy suppliers for machines, while their consciousness is entertained
and deceived by an artificial reality, the Matrix.

Translated with www.DeepL.com/Translator (free version)

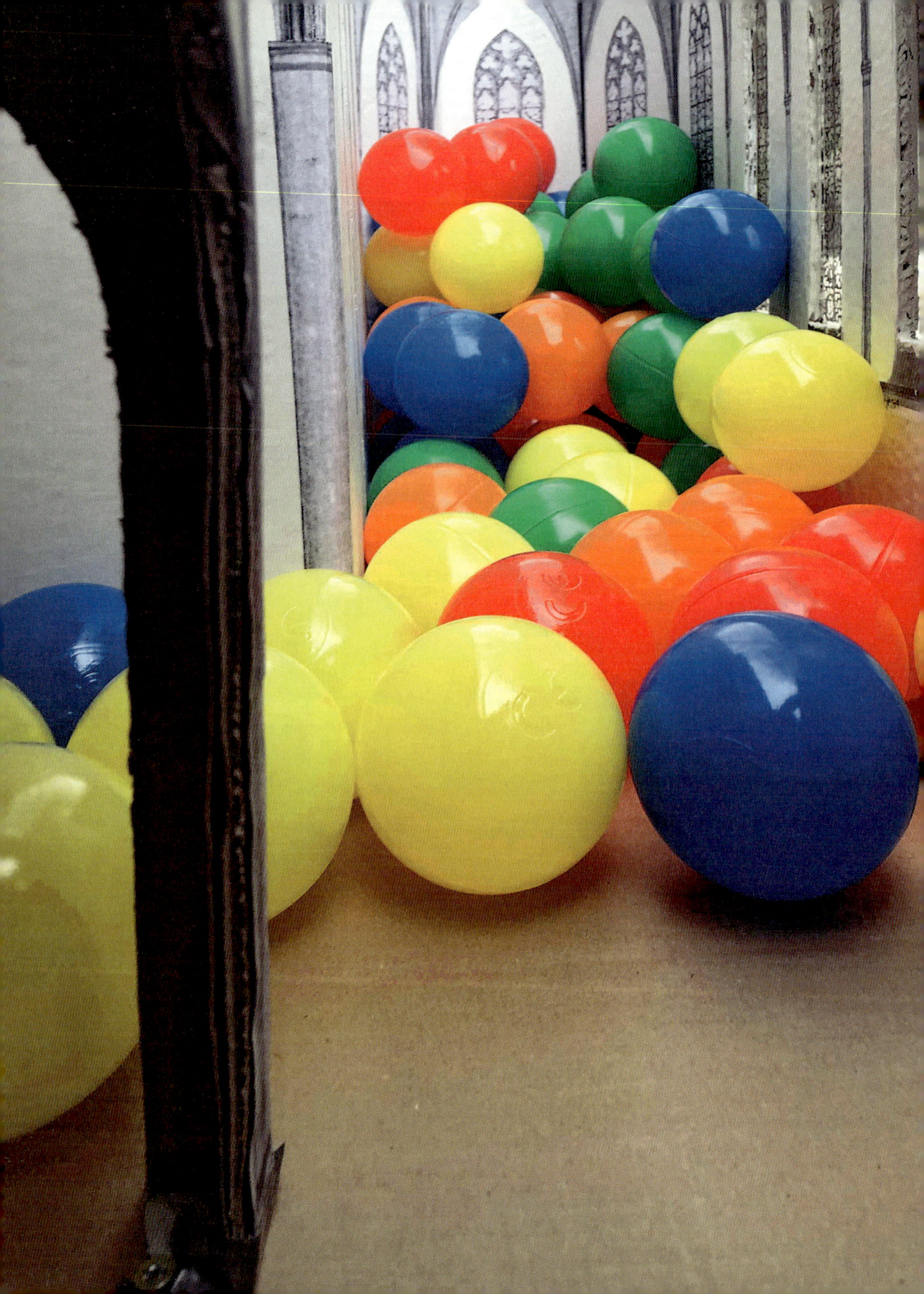

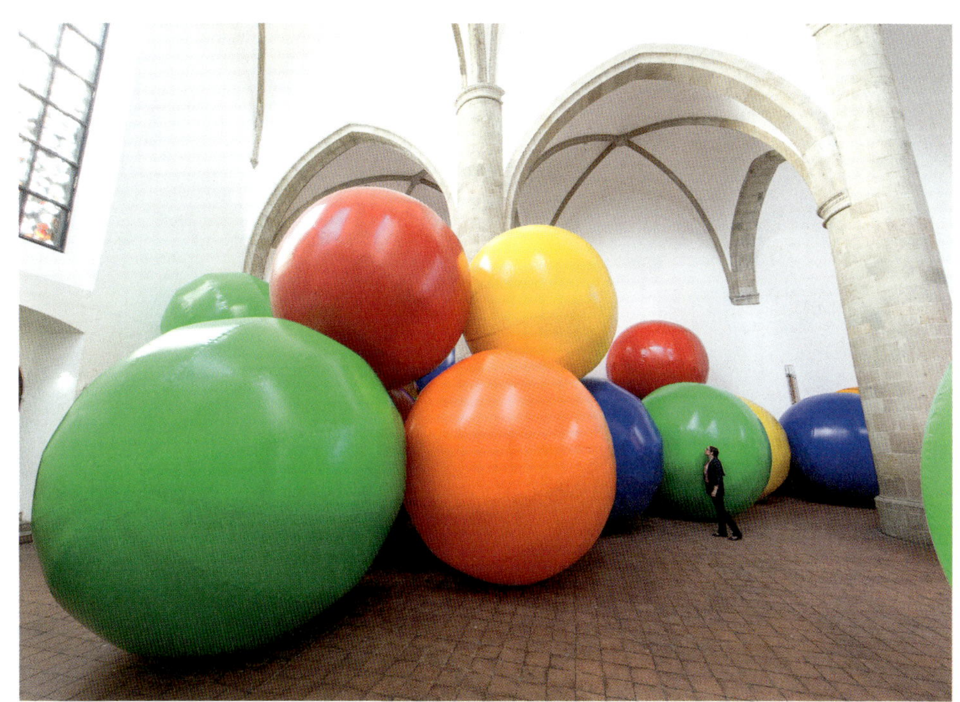

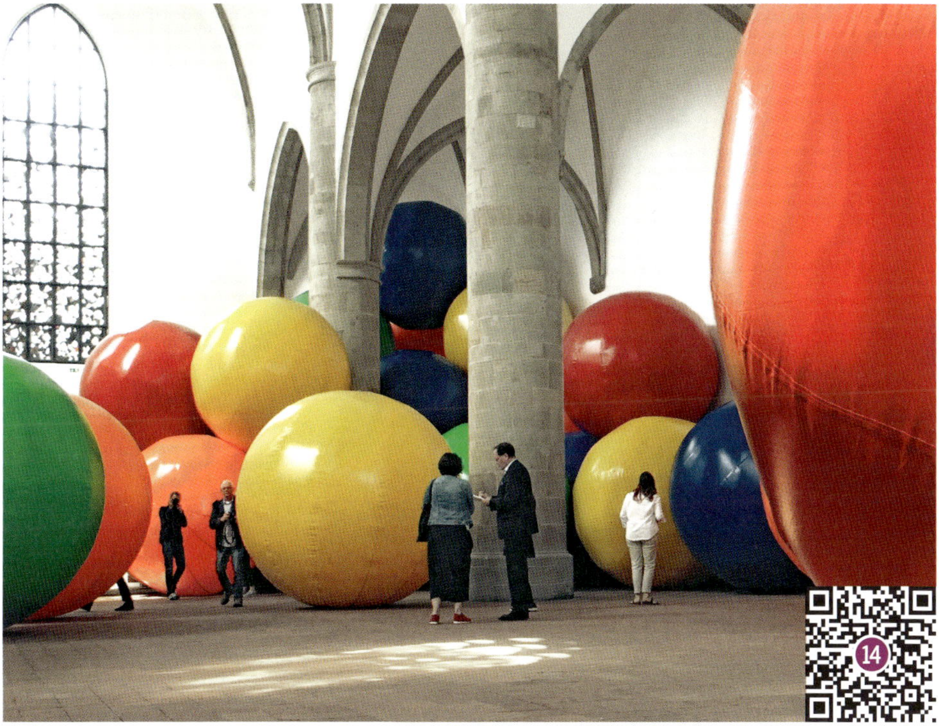

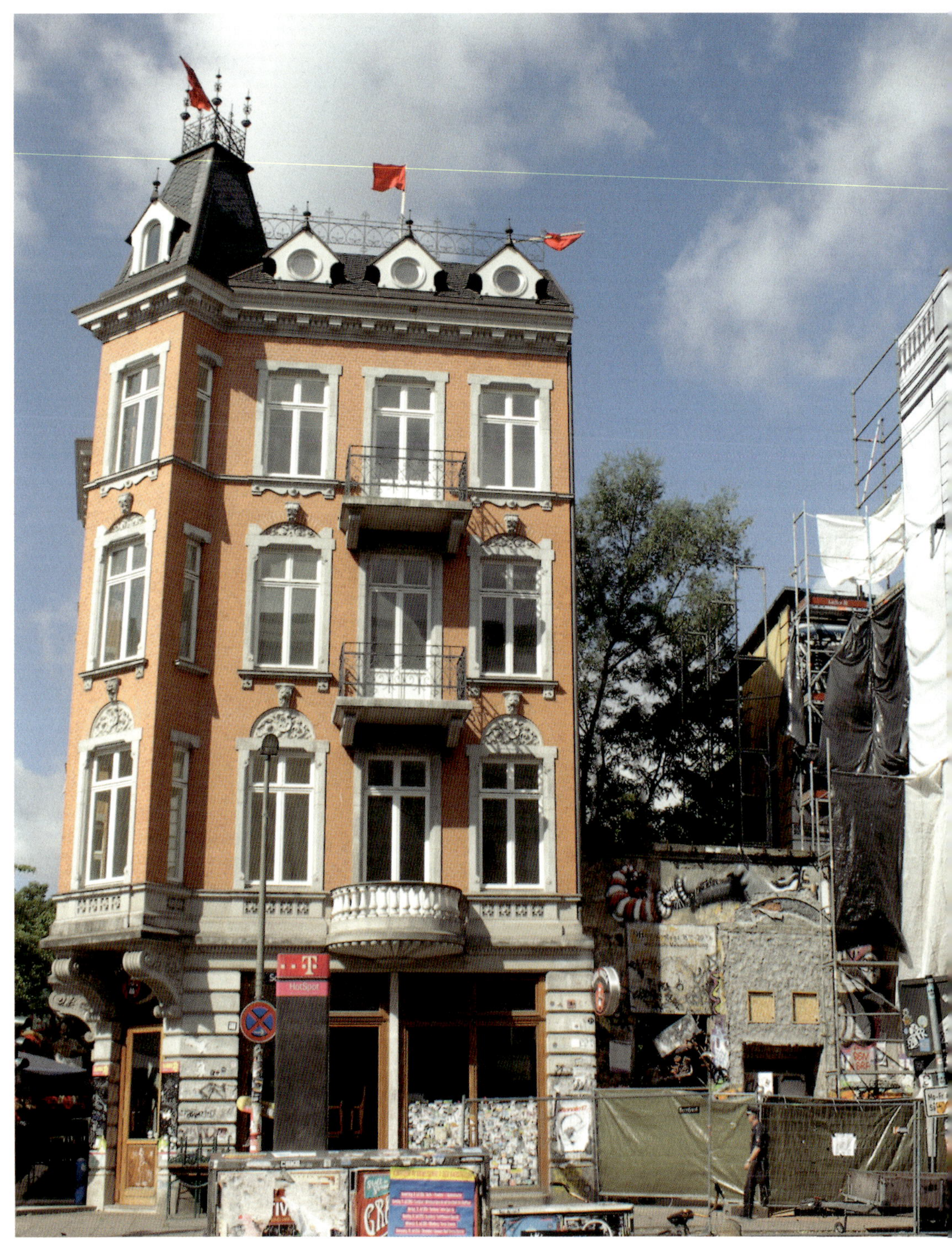

T
HotSpot

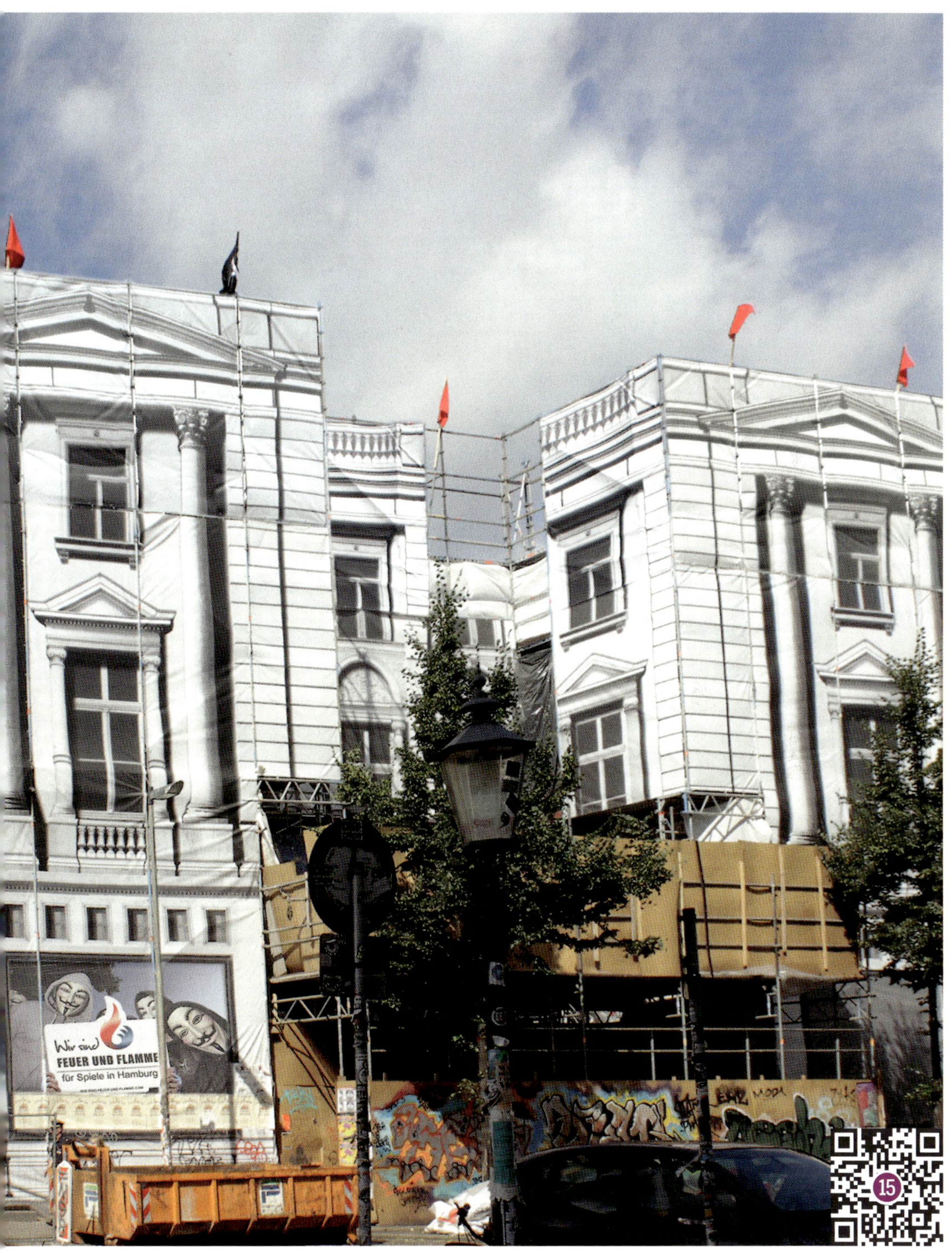

Wir sind
FEUER UND FLAMME
für Spiele in Hamburg

BILDER GEGEN BILDER. WIDERSPRUCH UND PROVOKATION IM ÖFFENTLICHEN RAUM
HOLGER KUBE VENTURA

Wie funktionieren Bilder, die den öffentlichen Raum und gesellschaftliche Konstellationen darin prägen und bestimmen – und mit welchen anderen Bildern könnte man ihr Funktionieren herausfordern und stören? Das ist eine Leitfrage im Œuvre von Christoph Faulhaber, der seine künstlerischen Aktionen und Interventionen der letzten fünfzehn Jahre in dem dokufiktionalen Film *Jedes Bild ist ein leeres Bild* (2014) chronologisch resümiert. Dabei ist ihm nicht nur ein Porträt seines bisherigen Schaffens gelungen, sondern auch ein neues, eigenständiges Werk, dessen inhaltliche und formale Dimensionen miteinander korrespondieren und dadurch zu etwas Drittem werden – ganz wie bei einem Künstlerbuch, das eben nicht nur frühere Arbeiten repräsentiert, sondern selbst ein künstlerisches Statement ist.

Christoph Faulhaber lässt in diesem Film sein künstlerisches Schaffen Revue passieren, hält inne und fragt sich: Was habe ich getan, wie kam eines zum anderen und wo führt der eingeschlagene Weg hin? Dabei wird die Rolle des Icherzählers zum größten Teil einer künstlichen Figur überlassen, die sich in einer dem Computerspiel *Grand Theft Auto IV* entlehnten Szenerie bewegt (es ist eine virtuelle Kopie New York Citys), zuweilen ergänzt durch Ausschnitte aus Martin Scorseses *Taxi Driver* (1976), und die das intellektuelle Alter Ego des Künstlers darstellt. Während dieser mit seinen Aktionen im öffentlichen Raum reale Mächte herausfordert, fragt sich das Alter Ego, welchen Sinn seine Abenteuersuche in der virtuellen Welt eigentlich hat. **16** Bei der seit 1997 sehr erfolgreichen Spielserie *Grand Theft Auto* (»schwerer Autodiebstahl«) steht bezeichnenderweise ein Protagonist mit krimineller Vorgeschichte im Zentrum, der in einer US-amerikanischen Großstadt eine Verbrecherkarriere anstrebt. Je schwieriger die von ihm übernommenen Aufträge sind – je mehr waghalsige Rennmanöver dabei bewältigt und Gegner abgeballert werden –, desto höhere Ebenen in der Verbrecherhierarchie kann der Spieler erreichen. Das Ende aber ist (wie bei allen Ego-Shooter-Spielen) von Anfang an klar: Man wird selbst erschossen, fährt vor die Wand oder stürzt vom Berg, es geht jedenfalls nicht weiter, und man muss von vorn beginnen. Und zu gewinnen gibt es – außer Score-Punkten und eventueller Aufmerksamkeit in der vernetzten Spielercommunity – sowieso nichts. Wäre dies auch das unweigerliche Los eines Künstlers im realen öffentlichen Raum?

Unterbrochen von den Sequenzen der virtuellen Begleitgeschichte erzählt und verknüpft *Jedes Bild ist ein leeres Bild* sukzessive Meilensteine der Projekthistorie von Christoph Faulhaber. 2001 strahlt der Künstler noch arglos in die auf ihn gerichteten Kameras, als er vom damals bekannten TV-Star Verona Feldbusch einen Preis für den besten Beitrag zu dem von Unilever ausgelobten Förderwettbewerb *Marken <–> Kunst* überreicht bekommt. Dieses Angeblickt-, Aufgezeichnet- und Zum-Bild-Werden lotet Faulhaber danach in seinem Projekt *Weltweite Musterung* (2001) **17** erstmals systematisch aus. Damals erscheint ihm das berühmte karierte Stoffmuster der hochpreisigen englischen Modemarke Burberry omnipräsent und bringt ihn auf die Idee, in

IMAGES VERSUS IMAGES: CONTRADICTION AND PROVOCATION IN PUBLIC SPACE
HOLGER KUBE VENTURA

How do images behave that influence and define public spaces and the social constellations therein—and what other images might one use to challenge and disrupt their behavior? This is a central question in the oeuvre of Christoph Faulhaber, who chronologically sums up his artistic performances and interventions of the last fifteen years in the docufiction film **Every Picture is an Empty Picture** *from 2014. In doing so, he not only succeeded in creating a portrait of his previous creative work, but also in producing a new, independent work whose content-related and formal dimensions correspond and thus become something else—just like an artist's book that not only represents earlier works but is in itself an artistic statement.*

In this film, Christoph Faulhaber recalls his creative work, pauses, and asks himself: What have I done, how did one thing come to another, and where does the path I have taken lead to? In the process, the role of the first-person narrator is for the most part left to an artificial character that moves within a scenario borrowed from the computer game **Grand Theft Auto IV** *(it is a virtual copy of New York City), occasionally supplemented by film clips from Martin Scorsese's movie* **Taxi Driver** *(1976), and represents the artist's intellectual alter ego. While with his actions in public space he challenges real powers, the alter ego asks himself what sense his quest for adventure actually makes in the virtual world.* ⓰ *In* **Grand Theft Auto**, *a series of very successful computer games first released in 1997, the focus is, tellingly, a protagonist with a criminal record who aspires to a career as a thug in a big American city. The more difficult the contracts he has accepted become—the higher the number of reckless racing maneuvers he masters in the process and opponents are bumped off—the higher the levels players can achieve in the criminal hierarchy are. However, the ending (as is the case for all ego shooter games) is clear from the outset: you get shot yourself, crash headlong into a wall, or fall off a cliff; in any case, you have to start over. And there is nothing to win anyway—except points and maybe attention in the networked player community. Would this also be the inevitable fate of an artist in real public space?*

Interrupted by the sequences of the accompanying virtual story, **Every Picture is an Empty Picture** *gives an account of and links successive milestones in Christoph Faulhaber's project history. In 2001, the artist still innocently beamed into the cameras pointed at him when Verona Feldbusch, a famous television star at the time, presented him with an award for the best contribution to the competition* **Brands <–> Art** *tendered by Unilever. Afterwards, Faulhaber systematically explored this being-looked-at, being-recorded, and becoming-an-image for the first time in his project* Burberry—Worldwide Grid ⓱ *from 2001. At the time, the famous tartan plaid pattern of the high-priced English fashion label Burberry seemed omnipresent to him and gave him the idea to beg, wearing precisely this*

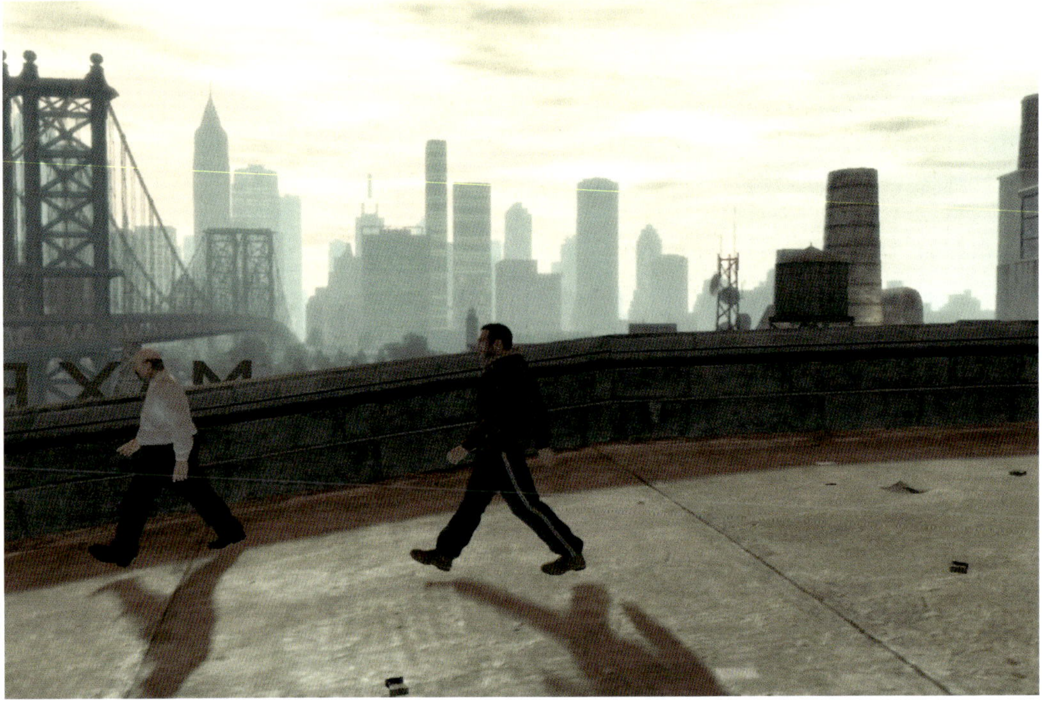

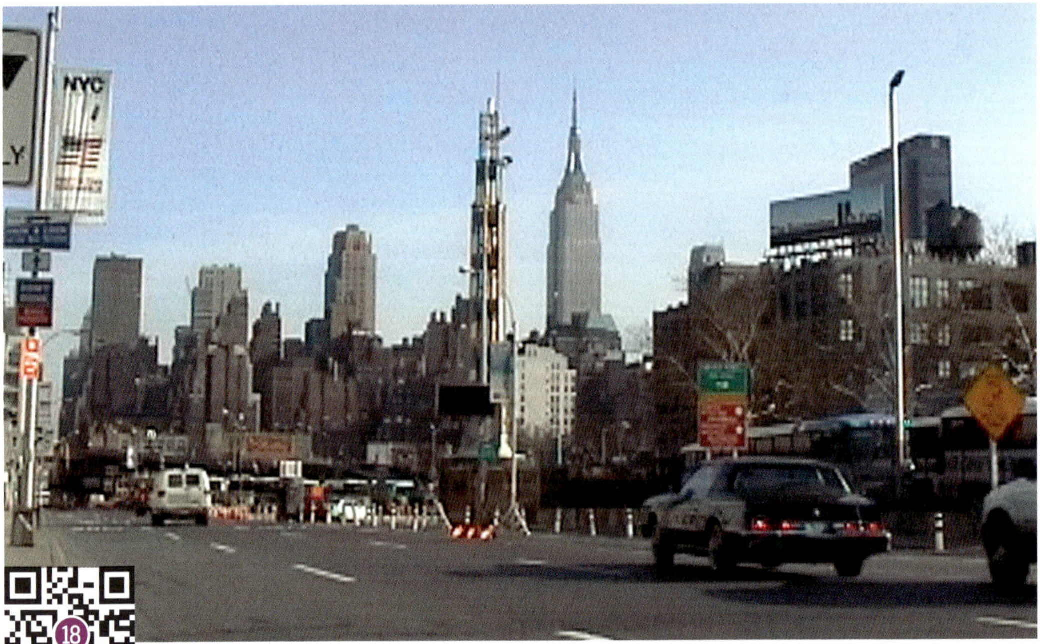

Der komplette Film *Jedes Bild ist ein leeres Bild* auf
*The whole movie **Every picture is an empty picture*** *at* guidedoc.tv | Promo-Code: **unbild**

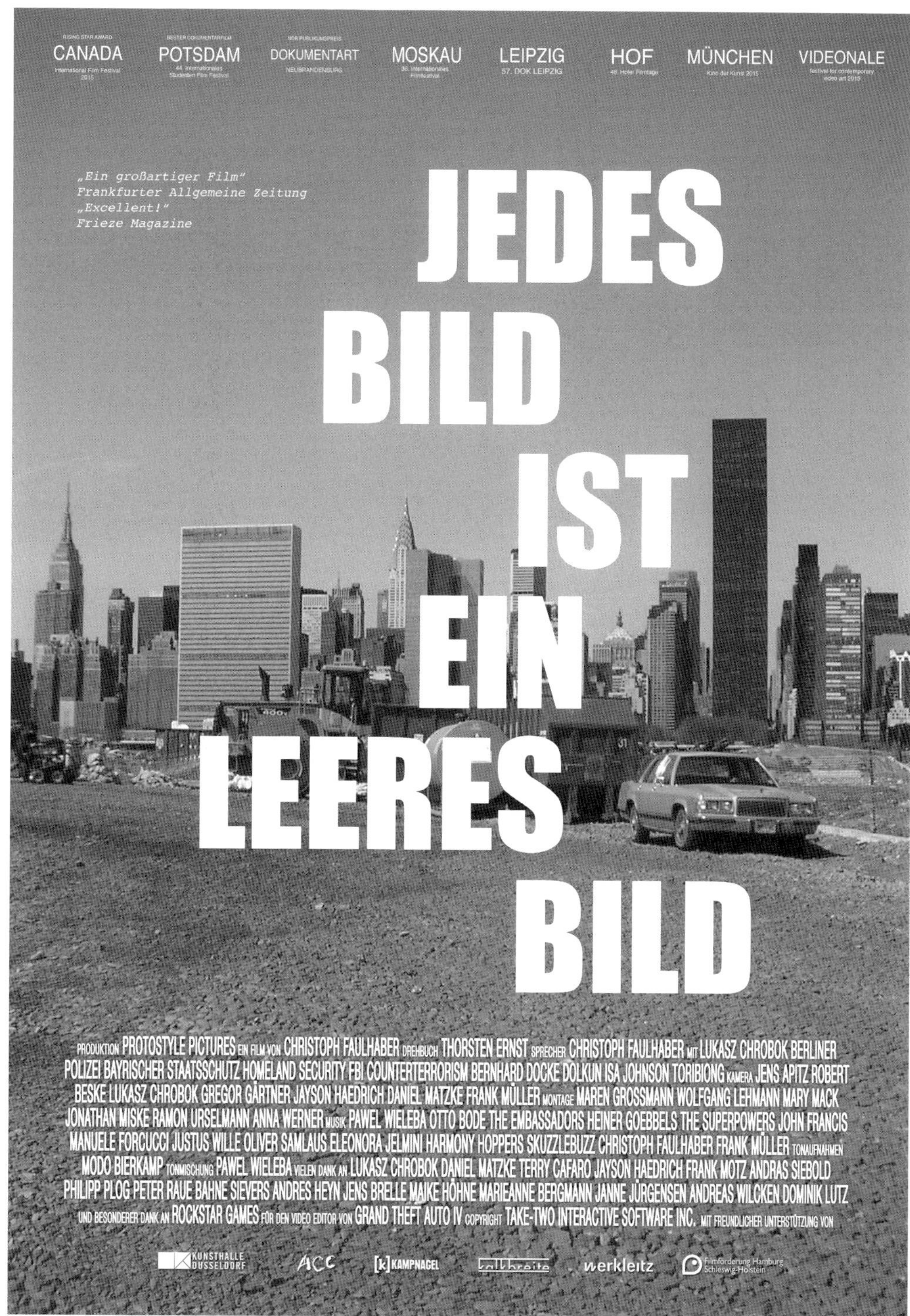
RISING STAR AWARD
CANADA
International Film Festival
2015

BESTER DOKUMENTARFILM
POTSDAM
44. Internationales
Studenten Film Festival

NDR PUBLIKUMSPREIS
DOKUMENTART
NEUBRANDENBURG

MOSKAU
36. Internationales
Filmfestival

LEIPZIG
57. DOK LEIPZIG

HOF
48. Hofer Filmtage

MÜNCHEN
Kino der Kunst 2015

VIDEONALE
festival for contemporary
video art 2015

„Ein großartiger Film"
Frankfurter Allgemeine Zeitung
„Excellent!"
Frieze Magazine

JEDES
BILD
IST
EIN
LEERES
BILD

PRODUKTION PROTOSTYLE PICTURES EIN FILM VON CHRISTOPH FAULHABER DREHBUCH THORSTEN ERNST SPRECHER CHRISTOPH FAULHABER MIT LUKASZ CHROBOK BERLINER POLIZEI BAYRISCHER STAATSSCHUTZ HOMELAND SECURITY FBI COUNTERTERRORISM BERNHARD DOCKE DOLKUN ISA JOHNSON TORIBIONG KAMERA JENS APITZ ROBERT BESKE LUKASZ CHROBOK GREGOR GÄRTNER JAYSON HAEDRICH DANIEL MATZKE FRANK MÜLLER MONTAGE MAREN GROSSMANN WOLFGANG LEHMANN MARY MACK JONATHAN MISKE RAMON URSELMANN ANNA WERNER MUSIK PAWEL WIELEBA OTTO BODE THE EMBASSADORS HEINER GOEBBELS THE SUPERPOWERS JOHN FRANCIS MANUELE FORCUCCI JUSTUS WILLE OLIVER SAMLAUS ELEONORA JELMINI HARMONY HOPPERS SKUZZLEBUZZ CHRISTOPH FAULHABER FRANK MÜLLER TONAUFNAHMEN MODO BIERKAMP TONMISCHUNG PAWEL WIELEBA VIELEN DANK AN LUKASZ CHROBOK DANIEL MATZKE TERRY CAFARO JAYSON HAEDRICH FRANK MOTZ ANDRAS SIEBOLD PHILIPP PLOG PETER RAUE BAHNE SIEVERS ANDRES HEYN JENS BRELLE MAIKE HÖHNE MARIEANNE BERGMANN JANNE JÜRGENSEN ANDREAS WILCKEN DOMINIK LUTZ UND BESONDERER DANK AN ROCKSTAR GAMES FÜR DEN VIDEO EDITOR VON GRAND THEFT AUTO IV COPYRIGHT TAKE-TWO INTERACTIVE SOFTWARE INC. MIT FREUNDLICHER UNTERSTÜTZUNG VON

KUNSTHALLE DÜSSELDORF   ACC   [k] KAMPNAGEL   vollbreite   werkleitz   Filmförderung Hamburg Schleswig-Holstein

mehreren europäischen Großstädten in ebendieses Muster gekleidet vor jenen Boutiquen zu betteln, die Burberry-Kleidung in ihren Schaufenstern anbieten. Im Selbstversuch soll herausgefunden werden, ob dieses konterkarierende Bild – also die sichtbare Aktion beziehungsweise Situation auf dem Bürgersteig – einen Konflikt herstellt und welche Bilder der öffentliche Raum einer Einkaufsmeile verträgt.

 19 Dafür war er nach New York gereist, um sich dort den zahlreichen Bürgerinitiativen anzuschließen, die über die Zukunft von Ground Zero und über Pläne zur Neubebauung und -gestaltung dieses Ortes berieten: Wie viel dieser nationalen Wunde darf und wie viel davon muss im Stadtbild von New York sichtbar bleiben? Bald darauf zogen die USA in den Krieg gegen den Irak, weil dieser »Schurkenstaat« den Terrorismus unterstütze und Massenvernichtungswaffen produziere. Als später der UN-Waffeninspektor David Kelly tot in einem Waldstück aufgefunden wurde, kurz bevor er seine Untersuchungen zu dieser Kriegsbegründung – die womöglich globalpolitische Auswirkungen gehabt hätten – veröffentlichen konnte, und es zeitgleich zu einem ebenfalls unaufgeklärten Waldbrand am Wohnort Christoph Faulhabers kam, wurde diese Koinzidenz zum Ausgangspunkt der Aktion/Videoinstallation des Künstlers *Die Geschichte wird uns vergeben* (2003). Faulhaber versuchte die verbrannte Erde im Wald durch Bewässerung mit einer Gartengießkanne zu heilen (und eine zufällig gefundene Plastikorange zu begraben), und das Video dieser Aktion wurde dann zum Zentrum einer Installation aus mit schwarzer Folie verpackten Möbeln eines Wohnzimmers, in dem man sonst vielleicht die täglichen Fernsehnachrichten anschauen und von Kellys Tod erfahren würde. Allzu schnell ist Gras über den Fall Kelly gewachsen.

2003 erhielt Christoph Faulhaber das *Stipendium für Kunst und Landschaft* im idyllisch gelegenen Landkreis Schaumburg nahe Hannover und realisierte dort wiederum ein Bild, das einen massiven Eingriff darstellte. Mit dem Auto walzte er in ein blühendes Rapsfeld eine Spur, die auf Luftaufnahmen – aber nur dort – als Autobahnkreuz lesbar gewesen wäre. Da solch eine Markierung *(Straßen gehören zur Landschaft,* 2003) in Stadthagen natürlich nicht den Vorstellungen von Landschaftskunst entsprach, gab es Ärger, und das Stipendium wurde nie wieder ausgeschrieben. Welche Bilder von Landschaften und öffentlichen Räumen also werden zugelassen, und wer darf mit Bildern diesen Raum mitgestalten?

 20 Als Angestellte von *Mister Security* verkleidet

pattern, in front of boutiques in several big European cities that displayed Burberry cloth-ing in their store windows. The purpose of this self-experiment was to find out whether this contradictory image—that is, the visible performance or situation on the sidewalk—produced a conflict and what images the public space of a shopping mile tolerates.

Ever since the terrorist attacks in New York on September 11, 2001, "it's been bombed into our consciousness that we live in a society of images" says Christoph Faulhaber in the voice-over of the transition to his next project **The Process** *from 2002, for which he traveled to New York.* ⓳ *Once there, he connected with numerous local initiatives that were discussing the future of Ground Zero and plans for the reconstruction and redevelop-ment of the site: How much of this national wound is allowed to, and how much of it must remain visible in the urban landscape of New York? Shortly thereafter, the United States went to war with Iraq, because this "rogue state" supported terrorism and produced weap-ons of mass destruction. When the United Nations weapons inspector David Kelly was later found dead in a piece of forest, shortly before he was to publish the results of his investigation into this justification of the war—which may have possibly had a global po-litical impact—and it came to a likewise unsolved forest fire where the artist lived, this coincidence became the point of departure for the performance/video installation* **Why People Set Fire (in Memoriam David Kelly)** *from 2003. Using a watering can, Faulhaber attempted to heal the scorched earth in the forest (and buried a plastic orange he acci-dentally came across), and the video of this performance then became the focal point of an installation comprised of living-room furniture packed in black sheeting in which one would otherwise perhaps watch the daily news on television and learn about Kelly's death. Dust had settled on the Kelly case all too quickly.*

In 2003, Christoph Faulhaber received the **Grant for Art and Landscape** *from the idyllically located district of Schaumburg near Hannover, where he in turn created an image that produced a stark contrast and was simply disruptive. With a car, he drove through a flowering canola field, leaving a track that would have only been recognizable as a freeway interchange in aerial photographs. Because in Schaumburg such a marking was naturally not commensurate with notions of landscape art, it caused a commotion, and the award was never announced again. What kinds of images of landscapes and pub-lic spaces are permitted, and who is allowed to help shape this space through images?*

For the momentous project **Mister Security** *(2005), Faulhaber and fellow artist Lukasz Chrobok founded a private security service of the same name with the self-mandated as-signment of monitoring and "securing"—whatever that meant—the tightly closed-off and yet in actual fact public space in front of American embassies.* ⓴ *Dressed as employees of* **Mister Security,** *they took pictures of the embassy in Berlin, and in a video that looks back at the performance, Faulhaber asks: "At which point does the camera become a weapon and the photograph become terror?" Real secu-rity personnel very quickly intervened—which was to be*

51

fotografierten die beiden die US-Botschaft in Berlin, und Faulhaber fragt in seinem rückblickenden Video dazu: »Ab wann wird die Kamera zur Waffe und das Bild zum Terror?« Sehr schnell — und das war vorherzusehen — schritten echte Sicherheitskräfte ein und Faulhaber bekam die Bilder, die er haben wollte: »Die Kamera soll einerseits Ursache der Reaktion sein und andererseits die Reaktion dokumentieren.«

In den folgenden Jahren erprobt und spielt Faulhaber *Mister Security* an weiteren Orten (Frankfurt, Hamburg, Leipzig, Warschau) und in verschiedenen Varianten. Mal wird ein Lieferwagen mit dem Motto »Wir überwachen alles« als mobiles Büro oder begehbarer Ausstellungsraum vor stark kontrollierten Orten oder vor dem Zentrum der documenta 12 (2007) abgestellt, mal wird ein fernsehreifer Videoclip gedreht, in dem *Mister Security* als Rapper auftritt und »Sicherheit« als coole Attitüde präsentiert. Die ästhetische Halbwertszeit solcher Clips ist kurz und Moden wandeln sich schnell, deswegen mag ein solches Rappen mit »security« damals Spaß gemacht haben, aus heutiger Sicht aber eher naiv wirken. Überhaupt nicht spaßig, weder damals noch heute, war jedenfalls das Nachspiel, das sich aus Faulhabers Provokationen bei den US-Botschaften ergeben sollte. Bei seiner nächsten Reise nach New York — dieses Mal als Residency-Stipendiat des Künstlerhauses Schloss Balmoral — wird er direkt nach der Landung am Flughafen von der Homeland Security verhört und bekommt später sogar noch Besuch von der Counterterrorism Division des FBI. Aus Angst, mit Leuten zu tun zu haben, die auf der Liste dieser Sicherheitsbehörde stehen, annulliert die Leiterin der New Yorker *Location One* Faulhabers Studioplatz, das Kultusministerium von Rheinland-Pfalz kündigt daraufhin das Stipendium und Faulhabers Vermieterin seine Wohnung. Später kommt ein vom Künstler eingeschalteter Anwalt zu dem Schluss, dass es deutsche Behörden gewesen sein müssen, die die US-amerikanischen über Faulhabers Aktionen vor Botschaften informiert haben, und zwar zu einem Zeitpunkt, wo sie diese bereits als Kunst anerkannt und somit als nicht strafbar bewertet hatten. Es gab also keinen Grund für eine Anzeige und auch kein — so der Behördenbegriff — »Sicherheitsbedürfnis«. **㉑**

In *Jedes Bild ist ein leeres Bild* ist es Faulhabers Alter Ego in der virtuellen Welt, das uns erzählt, wie im Jahr 2008 (übrigens genau während der Pleite der Investmentbank Lehman Brothers) die Lage des Künstlers in New York eskalierte und wie sehr ihm damals die geheimdienstlichen Repressionen zusetzten. Eingestreut wird aber auch ein kurzer Schnipsel aus der »realen« Medienwelt, wo man Faulhaber in einem der damals zahlreichen Interviews zu diesem deutsch-amerikanischen Überwachungsskandal selbstbewusst sagen hört: »Ich bin sicherlich nicht der erste Künstler, der auf dieser Terrorliste steht. Andererseits bin ich vielleicht schon der erste Künstler, der es darauf angelegt hat, auf diese Liste zu kommen« *(Ich wie es wirklich war, 2008/09)*. Stimmt das? Oder kann jemand, der sich mit solchen Mächten anlegt und deswegen natürlich jede auf ihn gerichtete Kamera nutzen muss, um den Kopf über Wasser zu halten, gar nichts anderes sagen? Erst Jahre später, nachdem der Presserummel um

52

expected—and Faulhaber got the pictures he wanted: "On the one hand, the camera was intended to be the cause of the reaction, and on the other hand document the reaction."

*In the ensuing years, Faulhaber tests and plays **Mister Security** at other locations (Frankfurt, Hamburg, Leipzig, Warsaw) and in different variations. One time a delivery truck with the motto "We monitor everything" that serves as a mobile office or an accessible exhibition space is parked in front of closely controlled sites or in front of the center of documenta 12 (2007), another time a video clip is shot that is fit for television in which **Mister Security** is a rapper and presents "security" as a cool attitude. The aesthetic half-life of such clips is short, and fashions come and go, which is why a rap number with "security" may have been fun at the time but from today's point of view comes across as naïve. In any case, what was not funny at all, either then or now, were the repercussions of Faulhaber's acts of provocation in front of American embassies. The next time he traveled to New York—this time on a residency scholarship from the **Künstlerhaus Schloss Balmoral**—immediately after landing at the airport he was interrogated by Homeland Security and later even received visitors from the FBI's Counterterrorism Division. For fear of having anything to do with people on the list of this security service, the director of New York's **Location One** annulled Faulhaber's studio, the ministry of culture of Rhineland-Palatinate cancelled the scholarship, and Faulhaber's landlady gave him notice to vacate his apartment. A lawyer the artist later engaged came to the conclusion that it must have been German authorities that informed the American authorities about Faulhaber's performances in front of the embassies, in fact at a point when they had already been acknowledged as being art and he was therefore not liable to prosecution. Hence there was no reason for filing charges, and neither was there any "need for security"—as it is referred to by officials.* ㉑

*In **Every Picture is an Empty Picture**, it is Faulhaber's alter ego in the virtual world that tells us how in 2008 (by the way, right when the investment bank Lehman Brothers went bankrupt) the artist's situation in New York escalates and how much the repressive measures taken by the intelligence service troubled him at the time. The video is interspersed with a short snippet from the "real" media world in which—in one of the numerous interviews on this German-American monitoring scandal—one hears Faulhaber self-confidently saying: "I'm surely not the first artist on this terror list. On the other hand, I might be the first artist who was out to get put on this list" (**I, the Truth**, 2008/09). Is this true? Or is it that someone who takes on such powers naturally has to use every camera aimed at him to keep his head above water and therefore cannot say anything else? It wasn't until years later, after the media hype about the concessions made by the Rhineland-Palatinate's ministry of culture had long since died down and the project was complete, that Faulhaber could apparently reflect on the affair in a more ambivalent way in his art film.*

Throwback to 2009; President Barack Obama wants to keep one of his campaign promises and close the notorious Guantánamo detention center.

das Einknicken des rheinland-pfälzischen Kultusministeriums sich längst gelegt hat und das Projekt abgeschlossen ist, kann Faulhaber in seinem Kunstfilm *Jedes Bild ist ein leeres Bild* offenbar ambivalenter darüber reflektieren.

2009 will US-Präsident Obama eines seiner Wahlkampfversprechen wahr machen und das berüchtigte Gefangenenlager Guantánamo schließen. Aber kein Land der Welt will die verbliebenen entrechteten 240 Insassen übernehmen. Daraufhin beginnt Christoph Faulhaber in Hamburg eine Kampagne und behauptet die Errichtung eines *Guantánamo Allocation Center – GAC* (2009) direkt in der neu erschlossenen Hafencity. Ein großes Schild weist auf das Aufnahmelager hin und stellt im öffentlichen Raum also wenigstens in bildlicher Form jene humanitäre Hilfe dar, die man von der politischen Führung ganz konkret erwartet hatte. Das Schicksal der Guantánamo-Häftlinge und die fast weltweit ausbleibende Hilfe steht auch bei Faulhabers folgendem Projekt im Zentrum. Er reist auf die Südseeinsel Palau, um dort einen Film über jene sechs Uiguren zu drehen, die vor ihrer Verfolgung in China nach Afghanistan und Pakistan geflohen waren, wo sie 2002 von Kopfgeldjägern an US-Truppen verkauft, von diesen nach Guantánamo entführt und 2010 nach Palau verbracht wurden – und seitdem die Insel nicht mehr verlassen können. Da sie nach wie vor überwacht und unter Druck gesetzt werden, kann Faulhaber keine Aufnahmen mit ihnen zusammen machen und zeichnet in seinem Film *Palau – Blue Sky* (2010/11) **22** deshalb das bizarre Bild eines gläsernen Gefängnisses mit unsichtbaren Opfern mitten in der Südsee. Dies ist die Stelle in Faulhabers *Jedes Bild ist ein leeres Bild*, wo sein virtuelles Alter Ego an einem Flughafen jede Flucht und Gegenwehr aufgibt und die Erschießung durch seine geheimen Verfolger hinnimmt – oder genauer: wo es von seinem Spieler Christoph Faulhaber nicht mehr gesteuert und also zum Abschuss freigegeben wird. Der Künstler scheint auszuprobieren, was Aufgeben heißt, und sinniert dazu aus dem Off: »Wahrscheinlich ist das Prinzip Scheitern ein Teil meiner Methode, zu arbeiten. Jedes Projekt beginnt mit einer Idee, einem groben Konzept, einem Versuchsaufbau, und dann lasse ich es laufen und gucke, was passiert. Der Widerstand gegen das Scheitern ist Teil der Arbeit des Künstlers. Form entsteht durch Widerstand.«

2010 reist Faulhaber nach China in das für seine Kopierwerkstätten bekannte Künstlerdorf Dafen in Shenzhen und lässt dort die von den sechs Uiguren erhaltenen Porträtfotos nachmalen. Es entstehen monumentale, realistisch gemalte Bilder in genau derselben Manier wie sonst die Porträts nach Fotovorlagen von etwa Mao Zedong oder Deng Xiaoping *(Palau Triptychon*, 2010/11). Somit können diese Uiguren durch das Transfermanöver des Künstlers wenigstens in Form großer Ehrenbilder nach China zurückkehren. Und Poster von diesen Bildern wurden fortan von Christoph Faulhaber in europäischen Städten wild auf den Straßen plakatiert – als Reintegration in den öffentlichen Raum, als Besetzung von Leerstellen und als Protest.

Die letzten Minuten von *Jedes Bild ist ein leeres Bild* widmet der Künstler einer Podiumsdiskussion aus dem Jahr 2013, bei der zur Debatte stand, ob die ursprüngliche Fas-

But there is no country in the world that wants to accommodate the remaining 240 disenfranchised detainees. Christoph Faulhaber subsequently begins a campaign in Hamburg and maintains that a **Guantánamo Allocation Center** *(2009) is to be built directly in the newly developed HafenCity. A large sign provides information about the reception camp and, at least in visual form, depicts in public space the humanitarian aid that one had expected in concrete terms from political leaders. Faulhaber's next project also focuses on the fate of the Guantánamo prisoners and the nearly worldwide absence of aid. He travels to the South Sea island of Palau for the purpose of shooting a film about six Uighurs who fled from persecution in China to Afghanistan and Pakistan, where in 2002 bounty hunters sold them to American forces who then carried them off to Guantánamo, from where they were taken to Palau in 2010—and have not been allowed to leave the island since. Because they continue to be monitored and placed under pressure, Faulhaber cannot shoot any footage of them and therefore draws a bizarre picture of a glass prison with invisible victims in the middle of the South Sea in his film* Palau—Blue Sky (2010/11). ㉒ *This is the point in Faulhaber's* **Every Picture is an Empty Picture** *at which his virtual alter ego gives up any thoughts of escape or resistance and accepts being shot by his secret pursuers—or to put it more precisely: at which he is no longer controlled by its player Christoph Faulhaber and he is allowed to be shot. The artist seems to be trying out what giving up means, and from off camera he muses: "Failure is probably a part of my working method. Each project begins with an idea, with a rough concept, with an experimental setup, and then I let it run and see what happens. Resistance to failure is a part of the work of an artist. Form develops through resistance."*

*In 2010, Faulhaber traveled to China to the artists' colony Dafen in Shenzhen, which is known for its copycat factories, and had paintings done of the portrait photographs he received from the Uighurs. What resulted were monumental, realistically painted pictures in exactly the same manner as portraits otherwise based on photographs of Mao Zedong or Deng Xiaoping (***Palau Triptych***, 2010/11). In this way, these Uighurs can at least return to China in the form of large-scale honorific portraits by means of the artist's transfer maneuver. And from then on, Christoph Faulhaber wildly pasted posters depicting these portraits in the streets of European cities—as reintegration into public space, as the occupation of blank spaces, as protest.*

The artist devotes the final minutes of **Every Picture is an Empty Picture** *to a panel discussion that took place in 2013 at which it was open to debate whether the original version of this film was allowed to be screened publicly, because Faulhaber did not have permission from the copyright holder of* **Grand Theft Auto**, *whose pictorial worlds (or video editor) he used in his film.* ㉓ *Today, when films are shot or photographs are taken in public space, then this can quickly bear on all kinds of copyrights by architects, rights to privacy, the trademark rights of randomly shot logos, and so on. However, when virtual realities, such*

sung dieses Films denn eigentlich öffentlich vorgeführt werden dürfe. Denn Faulhaber hat keine Genehmigung vom Rechteinhaber von *Grand Theft Auto*, dessen Bildwelten (beziehungsweise dessen Video Editor) in seinem Film zu benutzen. ㉓ Wenn heutzutage im öffentlichen Raum gefilmt oder fotografiert wird, dann sind davon schnell allerlei Urheberrechte von Architekturen tangiert, Personenrechte, Markenrechte von zufällig mitgefilmten Logos und so weiter. Wenn aber virtuelle Realitäten wie etwa das Setting eines Ego-Shooter-Spiels benutzt werden, dann gibt es sogar überhaupt kein Jenseits von Rechtsverletzungen mehr, denn noch der kleinste Ausschnitt davon hat stets vollumfänglich einen fremden Urheber. Damit schließt sich der Kreis in Faulhabers Film, den er zu Beginn mit folgenden Worten eingeleitet hatte: »Mehr als 50 Prozent unserer Gegenwart sind heute schon medial generiert. Wir leben in einer Welt der Bilder. [...] Wir brauchen eine neue Form der Erfahrung, die dem Subjekt wieder Geltung verschafft.«

Christoph Faulhaber sucht nach dem gesellschaftlichen Subjekt. Dazu sondiert er Grenzen zwischen öffentlichem und privatem Raum sowie zwischen realem und medialem Raum und zeigt, dass letzterer je nach Medium unterschiedliche Handlungs- und Projektionspotenziale aufweist. So erscheint es sehr konsequent, dass der Künstler seine eigene Projekthistorie in Analogie zu einer Episode in *Grand Theft Auto* erzählt und dort sein Alter Ego verortet. Sowohl in der Kunst von Faulhaber als auch in dem Videospiel geht es um die symbolische Eroberung von Stadträumen, und bei beiden könnte man zu der pessimistischen Lesart gelangen, dass der Akteur oder Spieler jeweils nur der Illusion aufsitzt, mit den eigenen spielerischen Interventionen zum Gestalter seiner eigenen Realität werden zu können. Wohin kann die bildhafte Spiegelung von Symptomen oder Regelhaftigkeiten führen, wie erhält solch ein Kurzschluss eine politische Dimension? Faulhaber konzentriert sich auf das Aufzeigen von Raumkontrolle, kann sich dabei selbst die Frage nach tatsächlicher Mitgestaltung einer unfassbar gewordenen Welt nicht beantworten und zieht deshalb daraus den – meiner Meinung nach falschen – Schluss, dass er kein politischer Künstler sei. Denn der Titel seines Films und seine letzten Worte darin sagen es ja genau, sie sind programmatisch zu verstehen: Jedes Bild ist ein leeres Bild. Das heißt: Jedes Bild kann oder muss erst gelesen, sichtbar gemacht, mit eigener Stellungnahme gefüllt und zum Ausgangspunkt eines anderen werden. ㉔ Das gilt insbesondere für Bilder von Gesellschaft, von Öffentlichkeit und den darin wirkenden Machtverhältnissen. Gerade bei diesen liegt im ästhetischen Lesen, Aufzeigen und Zur-Verhandlung-Aufrufen eine der zentralen politischen Dimensionen von Kunst.

Dieser Text wurde im August 2016 geschrieben und erschien erstmals in: *Christoph Faulhaber. A Golden Age*, hrsg. von Sabine Maria Schmidt, Berlin 2018, S. 128–132.

as, for instance, the setting of an ego shooter game, are used, then there is in fact no boundary to rights violations, because even the smallest detail always completely comes from an external originator. Hence Faulhaber's film, which he introduced with the following words, comes full circle: "Today, more than fifty percent of our here and now is media-generated. We live in a world of images. [...] We need a new form of experience that reasserts the subject."

*Christoph Faulhaber seeks the social subject. To this end, he sounds the boundary between public and private space as well as between real and media space and shows that the latter, depending on the medium, exhibits action and projection potential. Thus it seems very consistent that the artist relates his own project history by analogy with an episode from **Grand Theft Auto** and situates his alter ego there. Both Faulhaber's art as well as the video game deal with the symbolic conquest of urban spaces, and in both cases one could arrive at the pessimistic interpretation that the actor or player are each fooled by the illusion of being able to become the designer of their own reality through their own playful interventions. Where can the pictorial reflection of symptoms or regularities lead, how does creating such a short-circuit take on a political dimension? Faulhaber concentrates on calling attention to the control of space and yet cannot answer the question concerning the actual co-creation of a world that has become incomprehensible, therefore drawing what in my opinion is the wrong conclusion that he is not a political artist. For the title of his film and his final words in it say exactly that and are to be understood programmatically: "Every picture is an empty picture". This means: every image can or has to first be read, made visible, filled with one's own opinion, and become the origin of another. This applies in particular to images of society, of the public sphere, and of the power relations that operate therein.* **24** *It is precisely here that one of the crucial political dimensions of art lies in aesthetic reading, revealing, and calling for negotiation.*

---

*This text was written in August 2016 and was published in: **Christoph Faulhaber: A Golden Age**. Edited by S. M. Schmidt. Berlin, 2018, pp. 128–132.*

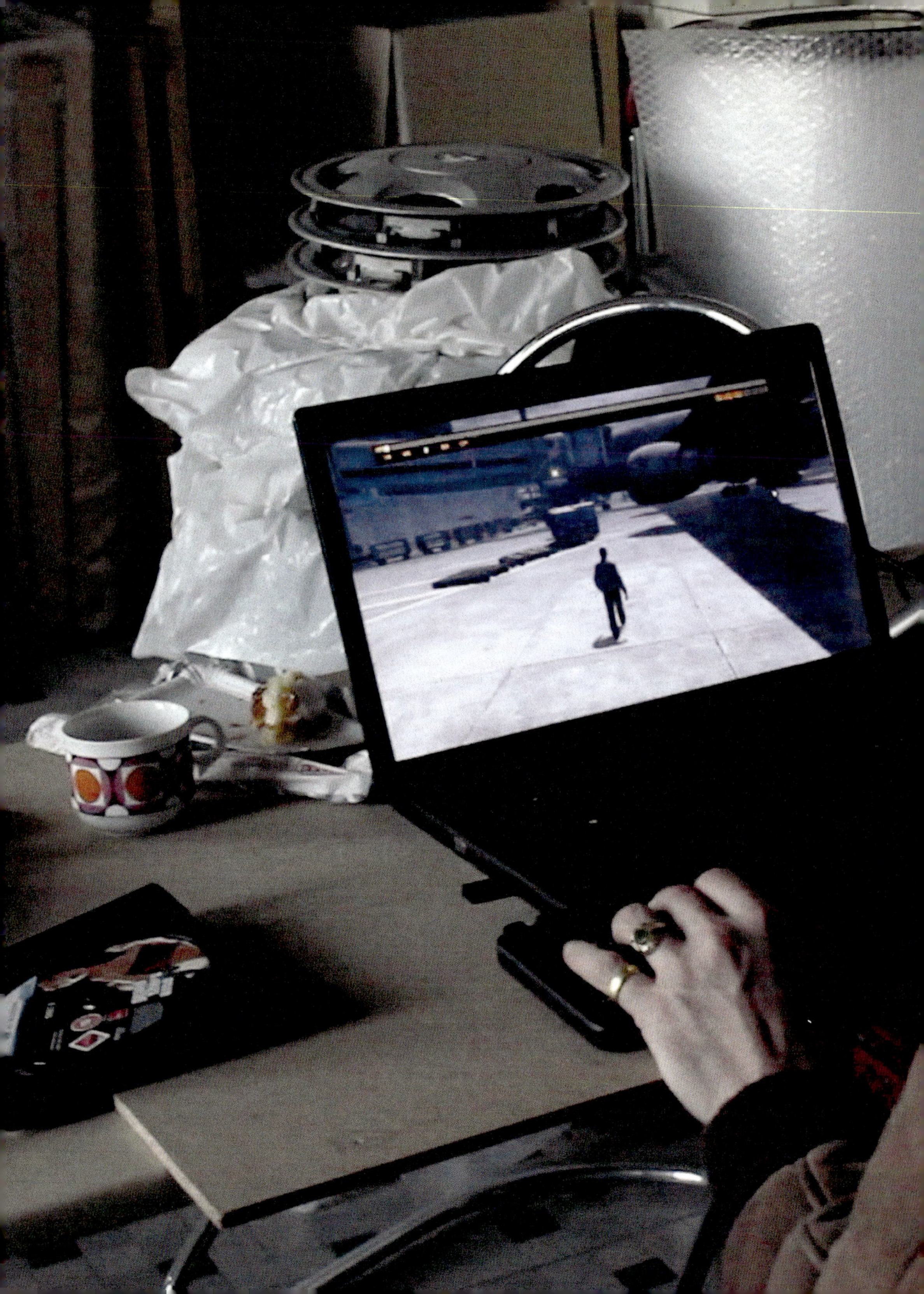

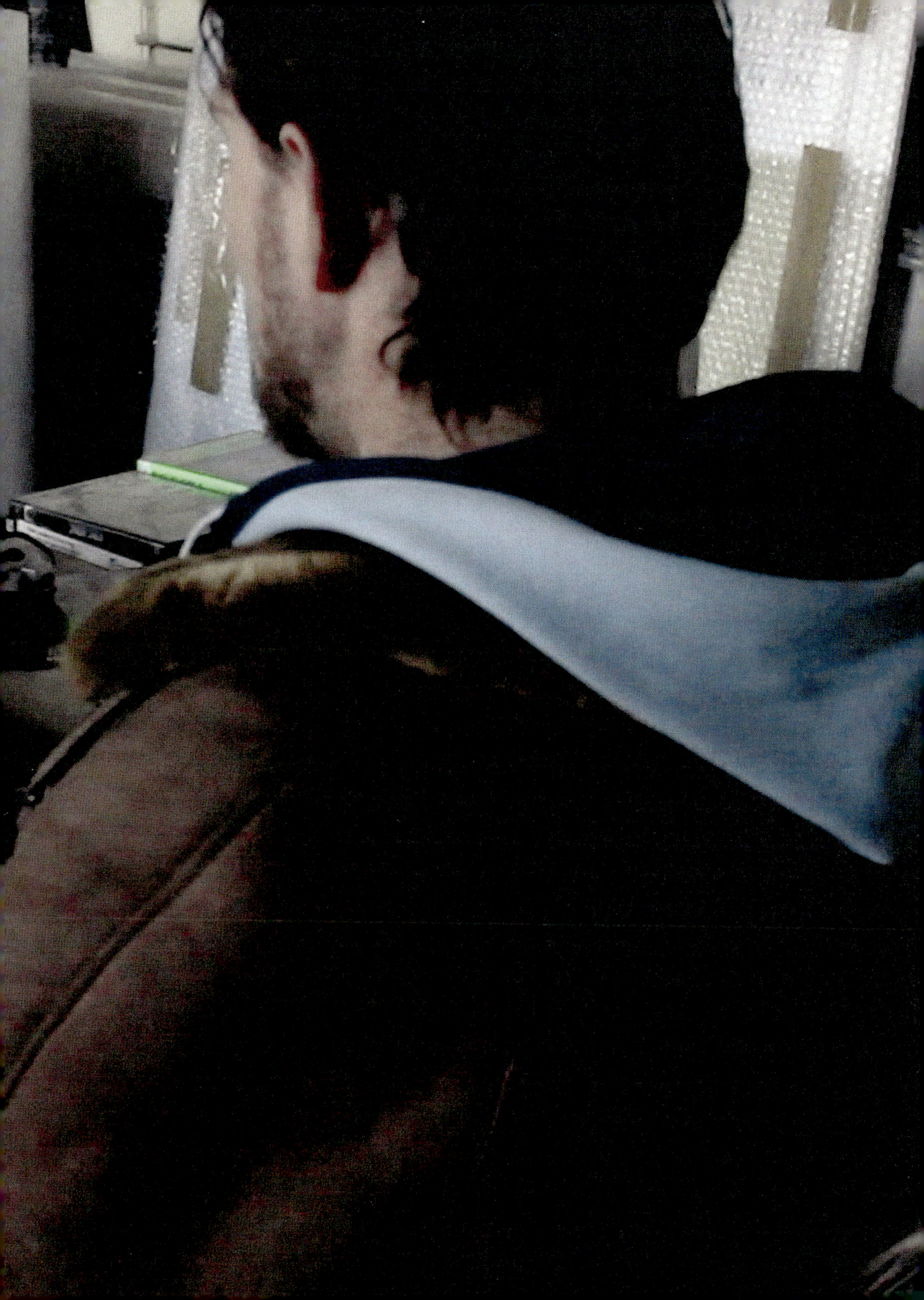

DIE AUTOREN

Inke Arns ist Kuratorin und Theoretikerin. Seit 2005 ist sie die künstlerische Leiterin des Hartware MedienKunstVereins in Dortmund. Sie hat zahlreiche Ausstellungen im Bereich der Medienkunst kuratiert. Zu ihren Publikationen gehören u. a. Studien über die slowenische NSK-Bewegung.

Alain Bieber ist ein deutsch-französischer Kulturmanager. Er ist der künstlerische Leiter des NRW-Forum Düsseldorf und Mitgründer von Rosy DX, Studio für digitale Transformation. Seit rund 20 Jahren organisiert er Ausstellungen mit zeitgenössischen Künstlerinnen und Künstlern, vor allem im Bereich Netz- und Medienkunst, Popkultur und Fotografie, die national und international für Furore sorgten, u. a. mit Jan Böhmermann, zu Algorithmen, künstlicher Intelligenz, Virtual Reality und Pizza.

Christoph Faulhaber ist Konzeptkünstler, Regisseur und Autor. Er ist für seine sozialen, politischen und gesellschaftskritischen Projekte bekannt. Seine Arbeiten wurden u. a. in der Schirn Kunsthalle Frankfurt, der Staatlichen Kunsthalle Baden-Baden, der Kunsthalle Osnabrück, im Museo Reina Sofía, Madrid, der Nationalgalerie Prag sowie in Mexiko, Lagos und Venedig präsentiert.

Andrian Kreye ist Journalist und Schriftsteller. Seit 2007 leitet er das Feuilleton der *Süddeutschen Zeitung.* Er ist Autor mehrerer Bücher und Filme. Von 1988 bis 2007 lebte er in New York und arbeitete von dort aus auch in Lateinamerika, Afrika, Asien und im Nahen Osten. 2019 erhielt er den Theodor-Wolff-Preis in der Kategorie »Thema des Jahres« für einen Beitrag über künstliche Intelligenz sowie den Medienethik-Award META.

Holger Kube Ventura ist Ausstellungsmacher, Kunstwissenschaftler, Kulturmanager und derzeit Leiter des Kunstmuseums Reutlingen / konkret. 2016 – 17 war er künstlerischer Vorstand der Stiftung Kunsthalle Tübingen, 2009 – 14 Direktor des Frankfurter Kunstvereins, 2004 – 09 Programmkoordinator der Kulturstiftung des Bundes, 2001 – 03 Direktor der Werkleitz Gesellschaft. Kube Ventura ist u. a. Autor der Studie *Politische Kunst Begriffe* (2002) und seit 1996 Initiator zahlreicher Großprojekte.

Lars Rummel ist freischaffender Kurator für immersive und interaktive Inhalte. Zur Zeit arbeitet er bei DOK Leipzig als Programmer der Ausstellung DOK Neuland und der XR-Konferenz DOK Exchange. In seiner Arbeit erkundet er Formen des Storytellings und versucht neue Medien als Kulturgut zu integrieren.

THE AUTHORS

Inke Arns is a curator and theorist. She has been the artistic director of Hartware Medien-KunstVerein since 2005, in Dortmund. Arns has curated numerous exhibitions, particularly in the field of media art. Her publications include studies of the Slovenian NSK movement.

Alain Bieber is a German-French cultural manager. He is the artistic director of the NRW-Forum Düsseldorf and co-founder of Rosy DX, studio for digital transformation. For about 20 years he has been organizing exhibitions with contemporary artists, especially in the field of net and media art, pop culture and photography, causing national and international sensation, among others with Jan Böhmermann, on algorithms, artificial intelligence, virtual reality, and pizza.

Christoph Faulhaber is a conceptual artist, director and author. He is known for his social, political and socio-critical projects. His works have been presented at the Schirn Kunsthalle Frankfurt, the State Art Gallery Baden-Baden, the Kunsthalle Osnabrück, the Museo Reina Sofía, Madrid, the National Gallery, Prague, as well as in Mexico, Lagos and Venice.

Andrian Kreye is a journalist and writer. He has been head of the feature section of the Süddeutsche Zeitung since 2007. He is the author of several books and films. From 1988 to 2007 he lived in New York and worked from there in Latin America, Africa, Asia and the Middle East. In 2019 he received the Theodor Wolff Prize in the category "Topic of the Year" for an article on artificial intelligence, as well as the media ethics award META.

Holger Kube Ventura is a curator, art scholar, cultural manager, and currently director of the Kunstmuseum Reutlingen / konkret. From 2016–17 he was artistic director of the Stiftung Kunsthalle Tübingen, 2009–14 director of the Frankfurter Kunstverein, 2004–09 program coordinator of the German Federal Cultural Foundation, 2001–03 director of the Werkleitz Gesellschaft. Kube Ventura is a.o. the author of the study Political Art Concepts (2002) and since 1996 has initiated numerous large-scale projects.

Lars Rummel is a freelance curator for immersive and interactive content. He is currently working at DOK Leipzig as programmer of the exhibition DOK Neuland and the XR conference DOK Exchange. In his work he explores forms of storytelling and tries to integrate new media as a cultural asset.

BILDNACHWEIS *CREDITS*

Covermotiv *Cover image:*
Christoph Faulhaber: Jedes Bild ist ein leeres Bild *Every picture is an empty picture,* Poster, 2014.
S. *pp.* 6—7:
Christoph Faulhaber: Diminish/Accelerate, 360°-Video, Video stills, 2020.
S. *pp.* 10—11:
Christoph Faulhaber: Diminish/Accelerate, 360°-Video, Video still, 2020.
S. *pp.* 16—17:
Christoph Faulhaber: AI Opera, Goethe-Institut Bangalore, 2019.
S. *pp.* 18—19:
Christoph Faulhaber: Alice + Bob,
2 Staubsaugerroboter, Farbmarker auf Leinwand *2 vacuum robots, paint marker on canvas,* 2020.
S. *p.* 21:
Alain Bieber im Gespräch mit Sophia *Alain Bieber in conversation with Sophia,*
Meta Marathon, NRW-Forum Düsseldorf, 2019.
 S. *pp.* 28—29:
Christoph Faulhaber: Alice, 1 Staubsaugerroboter, Acryl auf Leinwand *1 vacuum robot, acrylic on canvas,*
2020.
S. *pp.* 30—35:
Christoph Faulhaber: Diminish/Accelerate, 360°-Video, Video stills, 2020.
S. *p.* 42:
Christoph Faulhaber: #paradies *#paradise,* Modell *Model,* 2018.
S. *pp.* 43:
Christoph Faulhaber: #paradies *#paradise,* Installation, 80 farbige Bälle, Durchmesser 3 m
installation, 80 colored balls, diameter 3 m, Kunsthalle Osnabrück, 2018.
S. *pp.* 44—45:
Christoph Faulhaber: Phantom of Punk, Installation, Stahlgerüst, bedruckte PVC-Planen
Installation, scaffolding, printed PVC, Rote Flora Hamburg, 2015.
S. *pp.* 48—49, 58—59:
Christoph Faulhaber: Jedes Bild ist ein leeres Bild *Every picture is an empty picture,*
Film *Movie,* 72 min., Poster, Filmausschnitte *Stills,* 2014.

Alle Abbildungen von *All images by* Christoph Faulhaber,
außer *except:*
S. *p.* 21: Katja Illner
S. *p.* 43 oben *above:* Friso Gentsch / www.eye-work.com

Christoph Faulhaber. A Golden Age. Hrsg. von Sabine Maria Schmidt, Berlin 2018.

Mexibility. Estamos en la ciudad, no podemos salir de ella / We Are in the City, We Cannot Leave. Hrsg. von Friedrich von Borries und Moritz Ahlert, Ausst.-Kat. Goethe-Institut Mexiko + RM, Mexico City 2017.

Videonale.15. Festival for Contemporary Video Art. Hrsg. von Tasja Langenbach, Ausst.-Kat. und DVD, Berlin 2015.

Macht der Machtlosen / Power of the Powerless. Hrsg. von Johan Holten, Ausst.-Kat. Staatliche Kunsthalle Baden-Baden, Köln 2013.

Playing the City. Interviews. Hrsg. von Matthias Ulrich, Ausst.-Kat. Schirn Kunsthalle Frankfurt, Berlin 2012.

Christoph Faulhaber, **GAC — Guantanamo Aufnahme Lager.** Berlin 2012.

Theater Pößneck. Ein Sammelband. Hrsg. von Christoph Faulhaber und Dominik Lutz, Berlin 2011.

Art & Agenda. Political Art and Activism. Hrsg. von Robert Klanten u. a., Berlin 2011.

Playing the City 2. Hrsg. von Matthias Ulrich und Max Hollein, Ausst.-Kat. und DVD Schirn Kunsthalle Frankfurt, Berlin 2011.

Christoph Faulhaber, **New York, NY 10047/48. Der öffentliche Prozess des Wiederaufbaus des World Trade Centers nach dem 11. September 2001 / The Public Process of Rebuilding the World Trade Center after September 11, 2001**, Bielefeld 2010.

Christoph Faulhaber. Unbild//Projektkunst. An Introduction to Project Art. Hrsg. von Reinhard Spieler, Ausst.-Kat. »Das Leben der Bilder«, Rudolf-Scharpf-Galerie, Projektgalerie für junge Kunst des Wilhelm-Hack-Museums Ludwigshafen, Bielefeld 2010.

Oliver Zybok, **Christoph Faulhaber. Das Leben als Projekt. Ein Gespräch.** In: Kunstforum International, 205, November/Dezember 2010 (= Vom Ende der Demokratie), S. 152 — 165.

Christoph Faulhaber. Ich wie es wirklich war. Ein Bericht aus New York. Hrsg. von Oliver Zybok, Berlin 2009.

Hajo Schiff, **Christoph Faulhaber. Guantanamo Allocation Center.** In: Kunstforum International, 199, 2009 (= Existenz am Limit — Kunst und Klimawandel), S. 283.

ITCA — International Triennale of Contemporary Art 2008. Ausst.-Kat. Nationalgalerie Prag, Prag 2008.

Mister Security. To Serve and to Observe. Hrsg. von Oliver Zybok, Frankfurt am Main 2007.

Chrobok / Faulhaber. Cloning Terror Series. Hrsg. von Oliver Zybok, Frankfurt am Main 2007.

Christoph Faulhaber. Public Art 13. Hrsg. von Gustav V. Lhaba, Hamburg und München 2004.

Christoph Faulhaber. Kunsthalle Schaumburg: Alles muss raus! Hrsg. von Schaumburger Landschaft e. V., Bückeburg 2003.

Diese Publikation erscheint anlässlich
der Ausstellung *This book is published
in conjunction with the exhibition*
Christoph Faulhaber:
Diminish Accelerate: AI_VR_Games / Video
Galerie in der Wassermühle Trittau
28. März bis 10. Mai 2020
March 28 to May 10, 2020
AI Opera, Bangalore, Mumbai, 2020

Ausstellung und Publikation entstanden
im Rahmen des Kunststipendiums in der
*Exhibition and publication originated in
the scholarship at the*
Trittauer Wassermühle 2019/20
der Sparkassen-Kulturstiftung Stormarn
und wurden u. a. gefördert durch
and were supported by, among others
India Week 2019,
Freie und Hansestadt Hamburg,
Behörde für Kultur und Medien
Free and Hanseatic City of Hamburg,
Ministry of Culture and Media,
Goethe-Institut Max Mueller Bhavan, India,
Genossenschaft Kalkbreite, Zürich.

Herausgegeben von *Edited by:*
Christoph Faulhaber
Lektorat *Copyediting:*
Katha Schulte (Deutsch *German),*
Adis Begovic (Englisch *English)*
Texte von *Texts by:*
Inke Arns, Alain Bieber, Andrian Kreye,
Holger Kube Ventura, Lars Rummel
Übersetzungen *Translations:*
Rebecca van Dyck (Holger Kube Ventura),
DeepL, free version (Andrian Kreye, Lars Rummel)
Gestaltung und Satz *Graphic design and typesetting:*
Carsten Wittig, Leipzig
Herstellung *Production:*
Heidrun Zimmermann, Hatje Cantz
Druck und Buchbinderei *Printing and Binding:*
GRASPO CZ, Zlín (Czech Republic)
Papier *Paper:*
Magno Volume, 150 g/m^2

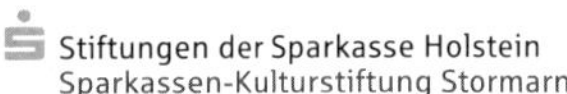

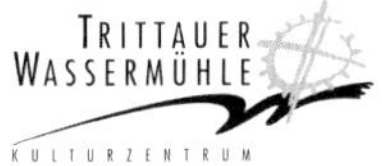
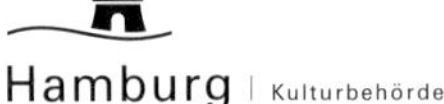
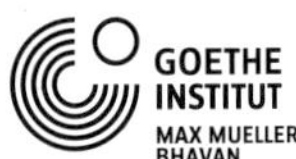
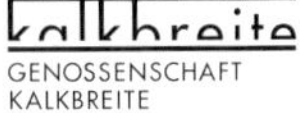

Erschienen im *Published by*
Hatje Cantz Verlag GmbH
Mommsenstrasse 27
10629 Berlin
Deutschland *Germany*
www.hatjecantz.com
Ein Unternehmen der Ganske Verlagsgruppe
A Ganske Publishing Group company

ISBN 978-3-7757-4717-2
Printed in Europe